11·95

Discovering Business

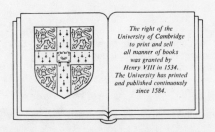

The right of the
University of Cambridge
to print and sell
all manner of books
was granted by
Henry VIII in 1534.
The University has printed
and published continuously
since 1584.

CAMBRIDGE UNIVERSITY PRESS

Cambridge

New York   New Rochelle

Melbourne   Sydney

Cover photograph by Nigel Luckhurst.

The authors and publisher would like to thank Nigel Luckhurst
(pp. (iv), 13) and David Simson/DAS Photo (pp. 1, 48a) for
permission to reproduce copyright material. We would also
like to thank Trevor Clifford (pp. 8, 39, 48b) and Peter Davidson
(pp. 19, 25, 35).

Published by the Press Syndicate of the University of Cambridge
The Pitt Building, Trumpington Street, Cambridge CB2 1RP
32 East 57th Street, New York, NY 10022, USA
10 Stamford Road, Oakleigh, Melbourne 3166, Australia

First published 1987

Published by permission of the Controller of Her Majesty's Stationery Office
Commissioned by the Manpower Services Commission
(Careers and Occupational Information Centre)

Printed in Great Britain at the University Press, Cambridge

British Library cataloguing in publication data

Discovering business.
  1. Small business – Great Britain – Management
  658'.022'0941   HD62.7

  ISBN 0 521 31004 0

G.O.

contents

introduction

Starting your own business may sound like a great idea but at the same time almost impossible. Or is it?

Anna, aged 20, is a market stall holder who makes and sells craft goods

I'd thought about starting my own business but thought it would be too difficult. Well, it was difficult to start with but not as difficult as I thought. I was surprised how many people were helpful.

I borrowed £300 from the bank to set up in the first place. This covered my new materials, equipment and workshop rent for the first month. I persuaded my bank manager to lend me the money by showing a business plan – a forecast of my sales and expenses for the first year.

Now I've got my business going and I really enjoy it. It's still hard work and I haven't exactly made a million yet but it's my business and I'm doing alright.

At weekends I plan my activities for each day. I write everything down in a diary otherwise I'd forget things.

I have three people making things for me but I make candles and shawls myself as well as taking out the stall. I had to get a permit from the city council for the stall. It costs me £28 a week.

I have set days at the market on Tuesdays, Thursdays and Saturdays. I get up early on these days, load my goods in the van and get to the market at least an hour before the customers so I can spend time putting on a display. I use a coloured backcloth so that my things stand out. I change the colour according to the seasons and to outshine my competitors. Presentation is important.

When I sell something I make a note of it and the price in my book. This helps me to keep a check on my stock and to keep an account of my sales. It also helps me plan.

Once a week I visit my suppliers to buy materials. I use two or three to get a good range of supplies at the best prices. It pays to shop around.

All my invoices and receipts are kept in envelopes marked for that month: June, July etc. At the end of the week it's easy for me to transfer the details of the money I've spent into my books. Twice a week I bank all the money I've made on the stall and transfer the details of my paying-in book into my own books at the end of the week.

I subscribe to three craft magazines to keep up with the current trends. They give me information about craft fairs which I take my stall to and I can also see which suppliers are giving special offers.

When I'm not out on the stall or seeing suppliers I'm in my workshop making up goods. I decided not to work at home, even though it would be cheaper, because I like the idea of 'going to work' and there are less distractions than at home.

Although it's hard keeping all the bits of the business working together, I wouldn't do anything else now except be my own boss.

About this book

Anna's story describes in a nutshell the right way to go about setting up on your own. This book goes into detail about the things she mentions. Anna had been on a self-employment training course designed especially for young people, and there are examples throughout this book of young people's experiences at different stages of their own enterprises.

This book is intended to be a taster of the main processes involved in setting up and running a small business. It is not possible to go into the finest details of every aspect – it is a starter pack for browsing, dipping into or for reference. It offers an easy level of explanation of the things you need to know to get started. The things to try out in the 'Do it' sections give you a feel for the processes of being self-employed and help you find out how suited or otherwise you might be. It is not rigorous, nor is it intended to be a test in any way. The intention is simply to guide you towards highlighting your own skills, aptitudes and temperament.

Discovering Business is intended primarily for young people in the later years of school, and on TVEI or CPVE schemes. Others on the Youth Training Scheme may also find it relevant to their studies, as may interested young people on further education courses, whether in college, in youth clubs, or in other groups.

Interested adults will find it an invaluable reference source too. It is written in plain language with easy-to-find sections and headings, and so can be enjoyably read by anyone.

How to use it

A glance at the contents list will show you that there is a logical sequence to follow in discovering business. But with any activity which involves organising, finding things out, and learning all at the same time, these processes overlap. For example, discovering how much people will pay may well happen at the same time, and influence what you will charge for your services or sales, as finding the right premises and discovering where you will work.

It might well come all at once and in a bit of a rush. So one way to prepare for that is to get an overview of the whole process. You can do that most easily by reading through the chapters in sequence, and trying the 'Do it' sections. You might skim over the bits you are more confident about, and spend longer over the ones you are not so sure about. Or you could use the contents list to pinpoint the bits you definitely feel are learning priorities for you and to select areas you want.

Because the process of discovering business is to some extent discovering things about yourself – your character, abilities, skills, etc. – you might get most out of the 'Do it' sections by trying them on your own. Afterwards, though, it would be valuable to discuss your responses with others, for example parents, interested friends, tutors.

If you are using this book on a course, you might prefer to use the 'Do it' sections in pairs or groups, though do remember it's your personal response that's important, not the group response. Afterwards, you can discuss it in detail with tutors and friends.

We hope you enjoy this book and find in it the things you want to know. We wish you every success in your ventures and adventures!

·DISCOVERING·
what you can do

Upholsterer, aged 19

I thought self-employment was a risky business. Well it is, but with so many of my mates being made redundant it seems that working for someone else can be risky too.

Working for yourself is no 9 to 5 job. It's frustrating sometimes and doing the paper work is boring. You've got to be a bit dedicated. I reckon it needs a bit of management and organising skill. I never thought I'd have that but it seems that I have. You've got to think about what you can do and whether people will pay for it. I was on a government training scheme that used to repair furniture for old people, children's homes, day centres and that sort of thing. When the scheme finished I'd already seen there was a demand and I could do the work. That's how I came to set up on my own. I do all sorts of furniture repair work and I have a special cheap service for old people and the unemployed.

Discovering your skills

Everyone has **skills**, **interests** and **knowledge**. You may not think of them in these terms, because you take them for granted.

It's a bit like driving. When you learn to drive there seem to be too many things to do and think about. There are the practical skills of changing gear, reversing, steering, etc. You have to concentrate on the hazards of the road and use your knowledge of traffic laws and road signs. You also have to keep your eye on other drivers. All these things have to be done at the same time! At first there seems to be so much to do that you think you'll never manage but after a while you find that you hardly have to think about it. You take these skills for granted.

If you take your skills, interests and knowledge for granted it can be difficult knowing what they are.

The rest of this section helps you to find out and think about these skills.
If you want to improve your skills here are some ideas to help you get started.

Evening classes

Find out about courses in your local college. Get a prospectus and ask someone in the general office to tell you what's on offer. When you go to evening classes you may still be able to draw unemployment benefit or continue to work while you are learning your skill.

Full-time college courses

Ask about these at your local library, careers office or Jobcentre. They will tell you which colleges run full-time courses in the skill you are interested in. You can apply for a grant for attending college full-time but grants are difficult to come by. If the course is less than 21 hours per week you can stay on unemployment or supplementary benefit. Ask about this at the DHSS.

Employment

You can try to find a job where you will learn the skill you require. If you do this you will be learning at your employer's pace rather than your own. You may also end up doing many routine tasks. But working for an employer will give you a realistic idea about business. You will have to do the day-to-day tasks as well as the exciting things. You'll also have the chance to see how all aspects of business fit together.

Youth Training Scheme

Ask at your school or local careers office about YTS. If you are between 16 and 19 you will receive an allowance while you train. There are a variety of schemes. Some help you learn work skills and discover what talents you have. Most will give you confidence and help you present yourself more effectively. All will give you the opportunity to try out practical skills and to become proficient at them.

Distance learning

Some types of skill may be learnt by reading about them and practising on your own. Distance learning courses are advertised in the national newspapers and in trade magazines. Look at *Second Chances for Adults* and *The Open Learning Directory* for more information (page 63).

Distance learning means learning with lessons you receive through the post, hence the term 'correspondence courses'. Correspondence colleges are a part of the education system that is always open to you – you never need entrance qualifications. All you need is the money to pay for your course and the determination to see it through.

Any correspondence college worth its salt will be **accredited**. That means it has a certificate from the Council for the Accreditation of Correspondence Colleges (page 72).

Some offer 'fast results', but in the end the only one who can get results is yourself. There isn't really any short cut; it's hard work, and often lonely. But you can at least work at your own pace, and at the time of day or night that suits you best.

Using your skills

Some people start businesses because they have a special skill or ability which they can use.

Paul:

'I'm a motor mechanic. I haven't got any qualifications to prove it but I've been repairing and rebuilding cars since I was about 14. I couldn't get a job in a garage because although I knew all about cars I had no formal qualifications. I started my own business from a rented garage near my parents' house. At first my customers were just friends. As word spread about my business being good, quick and cheaper than big garages my custom grew. I continued to work hard and to save money I earned. After five years I bought a house to renovate and a decent garage nearby for my business.'

For some people a hobby gives them the idea.

Sue:

'I do a lot of knitting and got the idea that since I spend so much money on wool it would be cheaper to learn to spin my own. I had to find out where to get spinning lessons and had to invest in a spinning wheel. I did all this for my own pleasure but realised that there was a market for hand spun and knitted garments. Three local craft shops offered to buy my garments or to sell them for a commission. I now spin and knit about two or three garments each week and can make a profit of about £70 each week.'

Here are two other ideas:

▷ Pete and Val set up a singing and dancing telegram business in London. Their overheads are low, it's fun and there's a lot of variety.

▷ Sally has a business selling fresh and dried flower arrangements. She supplies hotels, exhibitions and department stores with big or small displays for special occasions.

Of course, what you do depends partly on your skills.

There are more ideas in the 'Do it' section to help you think about your own skills and how you can use them.

3

Do it

Your skills

1 Write down 5 to 10 things you do, like sports, hobbies or just being with friends and going out.

For example:

Collecting records, fishing, going to discos, playing football, making models, using a home computer

2 Choose your favourite three and break them down – that is, divide the activity into the different things involved in doing it.

For example:

Activity	**What it involves**
Playing football	Using the ball: shooting, passing, dribbling, tackling
	Understanding the rules
	Being part of a team
	Training

3 Now break this list down further by thinking about the skills you need to do these things. You may take these for granted because they seem like common sense. But they *are* skills.

Here's how to do it:

What the activity involves	**Skills**
Being part of a team	Communicating
	Understanding instructions
	Getting on with people
	Helping others
	Understanding how others work/play

Do this with one or two of your activities.

4 Make a list of *your* skills under these headings:

Number	**Communication**	**Planning and problem-solving**	**Practical**
Think of things like:			
Working out the phone bill	Sorting out other people's difficulties	Fixing things	Fixing things
Using the cash dispenser at the bank	Making sure things happen on time	Making lists of things to do	Driving
	Organising an evening out	Making sure things happen on time	Using the cash dispenser at the bank
		Organising an evening out	

4

Which type of skills do you think you're strongest in? Make a chart with the headings **strong**, **OK**, **weak** and list your skills under these headings.

Which skills would you like to improve?

 5 Don't forget your special skills – from a job or special training, or your qualifications. Write down a separate list of these.

Your interests

You will already know what some of these are. But have you ever thought about the things that interest you which you've never quite got round to doing for some reason?

Write down ten things that you'd like to do one day.

If you were told that you could do five, but only five, which would they be? Tick them on your list.

This list should give you an idea of which things are most important to you. Do your five have anything in common? They may give you clues about what you might like to do in business. You are going to need dedication if you start your own business and it helps if you're doing something you enjoy.

Look at the next list: it will help you to sort out your likes and dislikes and also help you to define your strengths and weaker points. For each item in the list, decide whether you would manage easily, manage – but worry, just cope or not cope at all.

Being on your own
Working when friends have a party
Not seeing anyone you know for up to a week
Going shopping on your own
Working on your own
Travelling on your own
Being under pressure
Disciplining yourself
Organising other people
Working to a deadline
Having to do something new
Having to assess your own work
Working with strangers
Keeping appointments you are nervous about
Sticking with boring work

Finishing work that has taken a long time and that you don't like doing
Getting up in the morning
Working evenings and weekends
Meeting people you don't like

Handling other people
Giving other people praise when they deserve it
Telling other people what to do
Making conversation with people you don't know
Persuading people
Saying 'no' when someone wants you to do something you don't want to do
Asking someone to be quiet while you are working

Managing
Planning your time
Organising yourself
Finding the resources to do things
Dealing with people

Taking risks
Making decisions
Accepting changes
Moving to a new area to live
Trying out a completely new idea

From your responses you will get an idea of what you're good at and what you're not good at.

You could also get somebody who knows you well to have a look at your answers. Do they agree with how you see yourself?

Now you have thought about your own skills, interests, likes and dislikes, you should have an idea of what your strengths and weaknesses may be.

One of the secrets of having a successful business is to do something you like and which you're good at.

For example:

If you think that you're not very good at getting on with people, you're a bit shy and no good at persuading people, then selling may not be for you.

Your knowledge and special skills

Everyone has knowledge about certain things and often it comes with special skills. Often knowledge and skills are connected to interests. Could you use these for business purposes?

Here are some examples:

Knowledge/skill	Business use
Records and music	Starting a record stall, mobile disco
Computers	Designing or upgrading programmes
Books	Starting a book stall
Woodwork	Make simple furniture, doing woodwork repairs, building up a joinery business
Motorbikes	Doing up old bikes to resell or perhaps rebuilding bikes from scrap

Think of any special knowledge and skills you have and possible ways they could be applied to business. It doesn't matter how far-fetched the business idea sounds at first – some of the most successful businesses have started like that! Make a list with your knowledge and skills in the left-hand column and the business ideas they could be applied to in the right-hand column.

Remember the four headings for types of skills: number, communication, planning and problem-solving, practical. Here are ways in which you might think about these skills in relation to setting up a business.

Number
You will need some number skills in any sort of business.

Communication
If you're good at communication skills some of these might suit you: child-minding, selling, anything where you deal with people directly. You might make a good DJ if you set up your own mobile disco!

Planning and problem-solving
Being good at planning and problem-solving is important for organising your activities, planning your time and sorting things out.

Practical
Practical skills are useful in a small business. You will probably have to do a lot of things for yourself, for example repairing or making equipment, doing up premises, etc. Many of the 'practical skills' are things that have to be specially learnt, like decorating, painting, woodworking or gardening.

But we all know people that we would say are 'good with their hands' – people who are always making and repairing things – sewing, knitting, building things or fixing the car. All of these can be put to a business use. It depends what your practical skills are.

This chapter is about **interests**, and **skills** and **knowledge**. Here are some of the things you may have learnt:

▷   how to improve your skills
▷   how to know which skills you use when you do certain tasks
▷   what activities you really value
▷   some of your strengths and weaknesses
▷   more about your special knowledge
▷   new ways of looking at yourself

·DISCOVERING·
what people want

Renta Plant, aged 20

Customers are the key to business. No business can exist without them. You've either got to think of something people want that no one else provides, or find out what you can do that people will pay for.

Who would have thought there was a connection between offices and gardens? But I make a profit renting out plants to brighten up city offices.

Connections

Some business ideas take off when people connect things which aren't normally connected. Putting small plastic wheels on a flat board is an unusual connection. But the people who did it created skateboards and made a business worth millions.

Is there a connection between rising petrol prices and cycling? Many bicycle shops thought there was and sold a great many bicycles by publicising their cheapness compared with petrol prices.

Linking what people want with what you can do is called making connections.

The main part of this process is finding out. To make profitable connections you have to do some **market research**.

Market research

Market research is a business in itself. It makes connections as well. Some industries pay firms to find out what the public wants. Other firms have their own market research department. They do nationwide surveys to find out if people will buy a product, what they will pay for it, whether they like new products and if not, why not, and find 'gaps in the market' where people want something that no firm supplies.

8

Find out what market research is and what it's about by doing some for yourself. If you're going into business you'll need to know.

Help for market research

Whatever business you have in mind, a good source of help for market research, are the Trade Associations, for example the National Union of Small Shopkeepers and the Caterers Association.

Don't neglect your local library. They can put you in touch with organisations in your area. The consumer magazine *Which?* may be useful for finding out about competition for your business idea. Libraries usually have back copies. Find out about the product you are interested in producing and what big firms make.

The Department of Industry publishes *Business Monitors* four times a year. You can get this from H M Stationery Office. It has a huge amount of information from thousands of businesses all over the country who report on their progress. Much of it will only be of use to big businesses. But you may find it interesting and it will help you understand what market research and the performance of large firms is about.

The Government Statistical Service publishes a lot of books which cover a range of subjects that will be useful for market research. They are available from H M Stationery Office. Some may be useful for you so get a list of H M Stationery Office publications. Find the address at the end of the book.

1.   One way to tackle market research is to begin in your area.

   Ask yourself if you **really know** your area and what goes on there. Answer 'yes' or 'no' to the following questions:

   - Do you read your local paper daily/weekly?
   - Do you scan the small ads?
   - Do you know where your local library is?
   - Do you visit it more than once a month?
   - Do you know where the communication information is in your library?
   - Do you know where local community centres, old people's centres, drop-in centres, unemployment centres and youth centres are?
   - Do you know what goes on in them?
   - Do you participate in any local centres or use the facilities there?
   - Do you know what local firms and other organisations there are in your area?

○ Do you know something about the following list in your area: factories, housing estates, shops, clubs, small businesses, private houses, colleges and societies?

○ Do you know how big they are, how many people are employed there, what sort of age are they, what they do or provide?

If you have answered 'no' more than four times, you need to learn more about what's going on around you. Remember these people could be your customers. You should know, for example, approximately how many potential customers are male or female, middle-aged or young, wealthy, poor or average earners. You probably won't make much of a business out of repairing motorbikes if most of the local people are over sixty. But you could do a roaring trade offering a garden service!

2 If your knowledge about your local area isn't as good as you thought, try these suggestions for improving it:

○ Find out the addresses of all public organisations like the Citizens' Advice Bureau, colleges, Jobcentres, community centres and any others in your area.

○ Look at the shops. Are there already many selling one kind of thing — food, clothing, household goods — or is there a scarcity of particular shops?

○ How many people live on estates? How many in private houses? How many work in your area? Do they work in factories, shops, offices or small businesses?

○ Visit your local library. Ask the librarian to show you a detailed map of the area. Locate all the main buildings like schools, churches, hospitals and colleges. While you are in the library spend some time looking at the noticeboards. You will be surprised at the number of activities going on.

○ Visit the colleges, community centres and youth centres. Most will have large noticeboards which are open to the general public. See for yourself what they do in each place and also what is happening at other places in the area.

3 While you are building a picture of the area talk to as many people as you can. You may have some good ideas about what younger people want, but do you know what young mothers need, or old age pensioners, or middle-aged couples? They may have some ideas you hadn't thought of.

4 Make a plan of your local area marking all the important places. Think of all the businesses that could be connected with these places.

Using your plan, list what's going on and see if you recognise a 'gap in the market' — a need for something that isn't provided. Write another list alongside your plan of the type of business that may fill the gap. It might look something like the list opposite.

Shops

No record shop
No laundrette
No bookshop
only one greengrocer
No key cutting service
Only one restaurant - expensive
No hairdresser

Social

No community centre
Buses only run hourly
(taxi service)
Small Youth Club — no music
practice room
No organised child minders

Household

Few local gardeners
Window cleaners come from
next town
Car cleaning service?
Dog walking service?

Industry

No snack service
Cleaning services?
Printing facilities

5 Find a demand. Ask questions. You may find you can't look at a building without seeing a different business use for it, or at a shop without changing what it sells and the way it sells it, or at the way people work without thinking of better ways of doing things. Here are some questions you could start asking yourself about things in your local area.

- Could something in the area be changed? How?
- Is there a local demand for something?
- Is there something my neighbours need?
- Is there a lack of a particular type of shop?
- Is there a lack of particular types of services? For the old? For the young?
- Is there a different way of providing the services already offered?
- Can they be made faster, more efficient, friendlier?

6 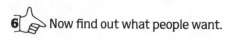 Now find out what people want.

Here is a sample questionnaire. You can change the questions to suit your own area and situation.

QUESTIONNAIRE

Name ....

Address ....

Age ....   Occupation ....

Do you live in this area?
Do you work in this area?
Are you happy with the number of shops in the area?
If you are not, what is your reason?

Are there any shops which you would like to see in the area that are not there already?
What are they?

Are there any household services (such as cleaning, mending, repair, etc.) that you would like?
What are they?

Do you think there is a good social life in the area?
If not, what social activities would you like to see?

Is there anything else you would like to have in the area?
What is it?

Progress report

This chapter is about making connections and doing market research. Here are some of the things you may have learnt:

▷   business ideas often develop by making connections – putting things together to provide a new product or service

▷   more about your area and local agencies, etc.

▷   how to do market research

▷   how to identify gaps in the market based on your own market research

3

how much to charge

Mohammed, aged 21

Indian cooking needs lots of herbs, spices and exotic ingredients. Many of my friends had mentioned that there were very few shops in the area that sold these things, so I opened a small shop selling them. I knew that my shop filled a gap in the market but couldn't figure out why business was doing so badly. Eventually, almost as a last resort I dropped the prices even though it would mean I hardly made any profit. My trade increased dramatically. Even though I make less profit on each thing I sell, I'm selling so much that I'm beginning to do quite well. My big mistake was charging too much.

Working out what to charge depends on two things:
▷ what you need to cover your costs, pay yourself and make a profit
▷ what people will pay

Here are some people's experiences of problems with costs and how they tackled them.

Carpenter, aged 21:

'I'm only starting in business. I've got all the carpentry skills I need but I haven't had much experience working on jobs. I like to check all my work to make sure it's up to scratch. Consequently I'm not as fast as a professional carpenter. So what I do is ask an experienced person how long it would take them to do a job, if it takes me longer I only charge for the time it should have taken me. This means I'm working for a very low wage. But it'll be worth it in the long run because I'll build up my business and get faster as I go along.'

Maker of fashion and home accessories, aged 19:

'All my bags and cushions and fancy linens were very expensive. I had to charge

13

much more than people were prepared to pay. They all took a long time to make. I was very fussy about finishing each item properly but when I looked at other goods in the shops I saw that they weren't finished half so well. Even though I didn't like doing it, I cut down on the time it took me to finish so I could bring down my labour costs.

I couldn't buy from wholesalers because I didn't have proper headed notepaper and couldn't order large quantities. Eventually I had some notepaper printed up and got a grant to buy £350 worth of materials in one go. Buying in bulk meant that it cost me a third of what it would have cost in the shops.

Jewellery maker, aged 19:

'I had a cheap workshop, but through the grapevine I heard of a watchmaker in the building. He was offering part of his workshop free to anyone who would take messages for him. I was so lucky. I'm saving more than £500 a year on rent, electricity and telephone bills.

Working out your costs

Your costs are made up of four main things:

Materials – equipment and tools

Overheads – regular costs like rent for premises or market stalls, rates, electricity and all the bills you have to pay just to stay in business

Your wage – think of yourself as an employee of your business; if you eventually employed another person it would be a cost to your business, so think of yourself as a cost as well

Your profit – how much you need to make your business grow

Materials

If you want to make a product, work out how much it costs in materials for a single item.

Write this figure down.

Overheads

Overheads are the costs, sometimes called fixed costs, that you have to pay to keep your business running whether or not it is doing well. They include things like rent and rates, electricity and insurance. They are called fixed costs because they vary only over a long period of time. This means you can plan for them and allocate money well in advance.

It is good business practice to know exactly what your overheads are. Write a list of every fixed cost you can and add up the running costs for your business each month for a year. For example, the total cost of bills for one year comes to

£1699. Find out the average monthly costs by dividing £1699 by 12.

$1699 \div 12 = £141.58$

Divide £141.58 by 4 to estimate your costs for one week.

$£141.58 \div 4 = £35.39$

£35.39 is what it will cost you just to run your business every week, whether you are selling anything or not. You must make at least this amount in order to cover your costs, before you make any profit.

The cost of your overheads should be counted in with the price of your product or service.

Work out how long it takes to make your product or provide your service. Then estimate how many hours you will be doing this per week.

If you want to work at least 40 hours every week, not all of this time will be spent actually making your product or providing your service. You will spend some time writing business letters, dealing with customers, or visiting suppliers among other things. So you might end up spending only 30 hours a week actually making or doing.

Divide your overhead costs by this figure. For instance, if your overhead costs are £35.39 per week and you produce actual goods or services for 30 hours per week, then you will work out the hourly overhead for your business.

$£35.39 \div 30 = £1.18$

This gives you £1.18 overhead costs for every hour you are producing goods or services.

If you are making a product which takes you half an hour to make, add half the overhead rate to the price of the goods. If you are providing a service that takes you four hours add four times the overhead rate to your price.

Your wage

The third thing to add to the price is your wage. Work out how much you need to earn a week. Be realistic. If you are just starting you can't afford to pay yourself a high wage. On the other hand don't under estimate your cost of living. If your business is to be a success it must be able to pay you enough to live on.

If you need to earn £50 per week, for example, remember that some time will not be spent actually making or producing a service. To work out your hourly rate you must divide the weekly wage by the hours you spend working. Let's assume again that you will spend 30 hours actually producing. Divide £50 by 30 hours.

$£50.00 \div 30 = £1.67$

This gives you an hourly labour rate of £1.67, so for every hour you are working on a job you charge £1.67 just for your time.

The final price you charge customers is worked out by adding the cost of your materials and your overhead rate to your wage, and then adding a bit extra for profit.

For example:

Your materials for one item cost £4.00, your overhead rate is £1.18, your hourly wage needs to be £1.67 and it takes you two hours to make your product. The final sum will look like this:

Materials	£4.00
Overhead rate × 2 hours	£2.36
Your wage × 2 hours	£3.34
	Total: £9.70

So to cover the cost of your materials, your overheads and your time you must charge £9.70 for your product.

If you only charged for materials, overheads and your wage there wouldn't be anything left over for buying or maintaining tools, hiring an employee, or getting bigger premises and so on. So you must add a bit extra as **profit**.

Your profit

This extra bit – profit – is important. You must make some profit but it is also the easiest part to cut down to begin with if you find people won't or can't pay what you ask.

Remember you will probably get more customers if your product is cheap. If you can sell two items with a profit of £1.30 each you will make more profit than selling one item with a profit of £2.00. But you must remember how long it takes to make each item. Two items with a profit of £1.30 each will make you more profit than one item at £2.00 profit. But you may have worked harder to make that extra 60p profit.

One way to find out how much your profit should be is to find out how much your competitors charge. If your price without profit is £9.45, and someone else making a similar product is charging £15.00, then you can add another £5.50 to your product and still be cheaper than your competitor.

If your competitor is charging only £12.00 for a similar item then you can only add another £2.50. If you add more your customers may go elsewhere because they know they can get it cheaper.

Cut your costs

What if your price works out much higher than your competitor's price? You may have to think of some ways to cut your costs.

Here are some suggestions:

o   Can you buy materials more cheaply? Perhaps you could use different materials or buy materials in bulk.

○ Could you buy equipment second-hand or hire or borrow it?

○ Can you save money on any of your overheads such as electricity, postage, gas, etc.? How?

○ Can you reduce the time it takes to do each job? Different equipment may speed up your work.

'Cost plus accounting'

The method outlined in this section is only one way of working out your costs and arriving at a price to charge. It is called 'cost plus accounting'. This means that you work out your basic costs and then add your profits and other costs to them.

You may discover that this way of working out what you charge isn't practical. For example, you may have to find out what people will pay and then decide if you can provide goods or services for that price.

Ask other small businesses how they worked things out.

Whatever method you use, the points outlined in this chapter will still have to be kept in mind – **materials**, **overheads**, **wages**, **time**, and **the customer's price**.

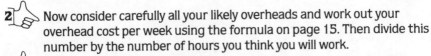

1 Think of a business that might be appropriate for you, and do a costs exercise for it. Use the examples in this last section to help you. Of course, you are estimating but try to be realistic.

These are some of the things to work out:

○ What sort of premises would you need? A market stall, a workshop, a room at home?

○ How much would this cost in your area? Think of ways in which you could find out this information, if you don't know already.

○ What equipment and materials would you need and how much would it cost?

2 Now consider carefully all your likely overheads and work out your overhead cost per week using the formula on page 15. Then divide this number by the number of hours you think you will work.

3 Work out what you need to earn as a wage in order to live. Consider these possible costs for your personal budget:

| Rent | Food | Entertainment |
| Clothes | Travel | Others |

Make a note of the total.

Divide this total by the number of hours you will work each week. Now add this hourly figure to the hourly figure of your costs.

This is what you need to charge for each hour you've worked in order to keep your business ticking over.

 4 What do you think would be a realistic profit to add to this?

What would this make the total price you would ask?

Do you think people will pay it?

If not, are there any ways you can cut your costs?

This chapter is about working out business costs, including your wage and how much to charge. Here are some things you have learnt:

▷ that costs are made up of three main things: materials, overheads and your wage

▷ how to think about these things if you set up a business and how to work out what your hourly costs may be

▷ something about profit

▷ what to charge the customer

▷ how to cut costs

·DISCOVERING·
where to work

Kevin, aged 22

I started my own joinery and woodworking business. At first I worked from a spare room in our flat. This was OK for a short time but problems soon started. The noise and the wood dust slowly spread through the flat and upset my parents. Then friends started calling during the day not realising I was working even though I was at home. The real problems started with wood being delivered and trying to take furniture I'd made out of the flat – it was chaos. I knew I had to find a workshop.

Organising premises

You could work in a corner of your bedroom or you could run your business in a building or part of a building that you rent or buy. How can you decide which will be best? The answer might depend on many things.

- o Do you need more space than you have at home?
- o Will you disturb your neighbours if you work at home?
- o Do you need **planning permission** if you work from home?
- o Will customers be coming to see you?
- o Is your home convenient for customers?
- o Are there many distractions at home?
- o Will you get lonely or bored if you work at home?
- o Will your family or the people you live with object to your working at home?
- o Is your home convenient for deliveries coming to you or your customers?
- o Do you need to have a shop in a busy area?
- o Do you need to be nearer your customers or your suppliers?
- o Will you be using heavy or large equipment which would be safer to use in different premises?

Your local authority or town hall may want you to apply for planning permission if you are changing the use of your home from private living accommodation to a business. If your business does not create a nuisance (for example, if it isn't smelly or noisy), they may let you continue without having planning permission.

Whether you decide to get premises or to work from home depends on your finances and type of business.

Some businesses need separate premises.
For example:

Warehousing – most homes would not be large enough
Shops – most homes are not in shopping areas and are too far away from customers
Printing – printing usually needs heavy equipment which would be unsuitable in most homes
Key cutting – the machinery used in key cutting is noisy and likely to disturb neighbours

Other businesses can be set up at home.
For example:

Dressmaking – is usually quiet and can be done in a fairly small space
Jewellery making – takes up very little room
Window cleaning – you would only need the use of a telephone and storage space for ladders and buckets
Childminding – involves only a small number of customers and a fairly small space, but you have to have lavatory facilities to register as a childminder (ask the advice or planning officer at the town hall)

If you need separate premises you have two questions to answer before you start looking:

How much money do you have?

It's no good saying you need a superb workshop in the centre of town if you only have £25 a week to spend on the rent. So you have to choose premises that you can afford. This will depend on how much money you can raise to start your business. You can find out more about this in Chapter 5.

Where do you need to work?

It's worth bearing in mind that when you first set up business you may not need elaborate premises. You may be able to manage with a garage or in very run down premises at first. You can always improve your premises once your business has got off the ground.

Finding premises

Wander up and down the roads in your area. Are there any empty premises?

Find out who owns the building. The council may be able to tell you if no-one else knows. Would the premises be suitable? If so, contact the owners to see if they are available for renting. If they look dilapidated you may get them for much cheaper than normal.

Visit estate agents

Explain what you're looking for. Give them an idea of the price you want to pay and the size of the place you are looking for. They may give you the key to empty premises so that you can visit them to see if they are suitable.

Look in the local papers

The adverts at the back often include business premises to let. Phone the number in the advert. Ask if you can visit.

Phone or visit your local council

The planning department of the local council usually has a list of all the empty premises it owns. If you are local and are doing something the council thinks is worthwhile, they may offer you a cheaper rent than you would normally have to pay. Some local councils offer grants towards the rent of premises. Ask for details of grants at the town hall.

Go to local organisations

Many large companies, charitable organisations or community groups have rooms to spare in their buildings. They may rent you space at a reduced rate.

Hidden extras

Before you decide on a place, check carefully to see whether it is going to need to be altered. This will cost money. You may have to alter the premises to comply with regulations. The main regulations are:

Planning

Ask the planning officer from the local council to tell you if you need planning permission to use the place for your business. It sometimes takes months to get an answer and you can't use the place until you get one. So be patient and persistent.

Health and safety

If there is loose electrical wiring or faulty floorboards you may have to pay to have repairs done. Your local health and safety officer will advise you. Phone your local council to contact the health and safety officer.

Fire regulations

All business premises must have adequate fire escapes and fire fighting equipment. Contact the fire officer at the town hall or your local fire brigade to find out if the premises abide by the fire regulations and what to do if they don't.

Fitting out premises

Once you've found premises you will need to fit them out for your business. You may need to carry out big alterations or, if you're lucky, just clean them up and add a few bits and pieces.

Here is a checklist of things you need:

Telephone   Water supply   Filing cabinet
Access to a lavatory Tables   Special lighting
Electricity   Chairs
Storage space   Workbench

Are there any more you may need for your business?

1. Which of these businesses do you think could be done at home and which would need separate premises?

Carpenter   Portrait painter   Woodturner
Fashion designer   Gardener   Watchmaker and
Motor mechanic   Photographer   repairer
Picture framer   Bicycle repairer   Magazine publisher
                   China restorer

2. If you have any business ideas write out the advantages and disadvantages of working at home for each idea. You could start with the list you made at the end of Chapter 1.

3. Here are some things to think about when deciding where your business premises should be. If you have any business ideas think about these points with your idea in mind. If you don't have any particular business ideas think about how these points might relate to different types of businesses.

Will you need:

- ○ to be near a main shopping area?
- ○ to be near a railway station?
- ○ to have access for a van or car?
- ○ to have smart premises?
- ○ to have premises in a fashionable or popular area?
- ○ to have your customers visit your premises?
- ○ to be near your home?
- ○ to have large premises?
- ○ to have small premises?

4. Look for premises for your business. The methods outlined on page 21 will help you. Can you think of other methods?

5 Make a chart of possible premises. Compare the benefits and disadvantages.

Your chart might look like this:

	Address	Size (sq ft)	Price	Access	Owner	Comments
1.	Acorn Studios 1 Napier Court	400	£50 pw	Main shopping area ½ ml from stn. Delivery bay at back.	J Thomas	Shop front, plenty of storage
2.	44 London Road	600	£35 pw	Edge of town on main road.	Kirkwood Warehouses Limited	In basement, smells a bit damp.
3.	63 Edgebaston St	350	£25 pw	Small side road near town centre. No parking, difficult for deliveries.	Local Council	2nd floor, light and airy, sink and workbench incl.
4.	24 River St	400	£30 pw	Quiet industrial estate near main road, easy parking and access.	Empire Stores Mechanics	2 miles from town. Next to noisy factory. Includes gas and electricity.

6 This is a plan of a workshop for a signwriter. How could you improve it?

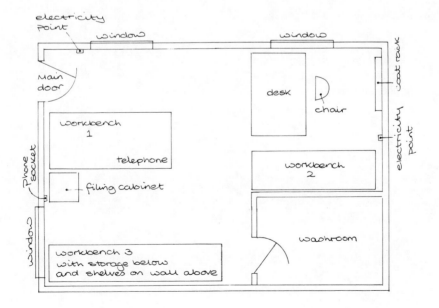

7 If the signwriter's workshop were available for renting, how would you alter it for different business purposes?

Think of your own favourite business idea. What changes would you make to the workshop?

Copy the plan on a piece of paper and decide what other equipment you would need. Mark where you would put everything on the plan.

How would you alter the workshop if you wanted it for:

o   a potter's workshop with a kiln?

o   a clothes-making workshop for two people?

8 Draw a plan of your ideal premises or workshop. Include details of where you will store your stock, tools and equipment.

Match this with the premises you have seen. Will any of them be suitable?

This chapter is about deciding where to work. Here are some of the things you may have learnt:

▷   some advantages and risks of running a business from home

▷   how much you can spend on premises

▷   where your workplace should be and what you will need in it

▷   some ways of looking for premises and organisations that may help you

·DISCOVERING·
money

The first thing you need to start a business is money. If you haven't got much money don't give up. Few people who start businesses have all the money they need in the beginning.

You can raise money. It's not easy but it can be done.

Jenny, aged 20

Since I was 17 I'd been a waitress in a restaurant. I'd always wanted to have my own clothes shop. When I was 19, I noticed a small shop premises for rent in a reasonably good shopping area. The rent was £100 per month. I said to myself, 'It's now or never Jenny' and set out to raise the money I'd need.

I reckoned I'd need about £1 500 for my initial stock and to pay rent for the first five months. I figured it would take that long before my business could pay the rent from its own earnings. I would also need about £250 for shop fittings, clothes racks and stationery, and at least another £250 for unexpected costs and bills. That meant I needed about £2 000.

I had £350 in my savings. I looked around to see what I could sell – and sold my bicycle, a radio, some records and some other odds and ends through adverts in the local paper. That raised another £150. This convinced my parents I was serious about the venture. After a lot of persuading my father agreed to lend me £300 and shortly after that he gave me £100. It was his way of wishing me well. I'd raised £900.

Then I went to see my grandad. He gave me £50 and loaned me £200 interest free. I think he was pleased to see me trying so hard. As word got around the family I got an offer from a cousin, who is a joiner, to help me to build some clothes racks and so on. Another relative who owns a shop gave me an old till that she used to use before she bought an electric till. This was really good because I wouldn't need all of the £250 I'd reckoned on for all this.

Now I only needed about £650 so I took the plunge and went along to the bank. I had to explain my plan in great detail but the bank manager was very helpful and nice. He agreed a loan of £800, mostly because he was impressed by how determined I was and how I'd managed to raise so much already. So I started out with a little bit more money than I'd originally figured on.

Help in raising money

It's surprising how many people and organisations may be able to offer money to help you start your business. You will probably have to provide full details of your business plans for people to examine. Read more about this on page 28.

Here are some suggestions:

Friends and relatives

A lot of small businesses start up on money borrowed from friends or relatives. This can be very helpful because friends and relatives may not ask for interest (extra money to be paid back as well as the original amount) and they may not set a time when the loan has to be paid back. A bank will do both these things.

But the risks are that friends and relatives may feel they can interfere in your business because they lent you money. If anything goes wrong with the business, and you lose money, you could fall out with friends or relatives.

A partner

You may have a friend or acquaintance who is willing to put up money for the business in exchange for being a partner. If you find a partner you should see a solicitor, who will draw up a legal contract stating the terms of your partnership. In some partnerships both people (or more than two people) participate in the day-to-day running of the business. In others only one person runs the business and the other partner only takes part in major decisions.

The risks are that friends don't always make good business partners. What if your partner continually disagrees with your ideas? What happens if, once your business begins to show a profit, your partner decides to pull out and sell up? You may want it to be your business and nobody else's.

Bank managers

Loans from banks are not necessarily as difficult to get as you may think. Possibly the most usual place to go for money is a bank.

▷   they'll give you professional advice
▷   they will want to see your business plan first and, if they agree to lend you the money, it may mean they think your business has a good chance of succeeding

You don't have to go to your own bank. You can try any bank. If you get turned down at one, try another and another until you find a sympathetic bank manager. Remember that a bank loan will cost you more than just the money you borrow because of the interest. Banks are businesses too and that's one of the ways they make money.

Sponsors and large companies

A sponsor is an organisation or individual who gives you money or other resources like premises, equipment, furniture or stationery. Sometimes sponsors or companies will give or lend you money if they are interested in what you're doing. Occasionally they will donate money in exchange for a service or advertising in your premises or to your customers.

Look in your local papers to see if there are any local sponsors who give to other businesses. Try approaching a few large companies in your area.

Agencies

Agencies will often put you in contact with potential sponsors. They will act as agents between a business starter and someone who has money to put into a business.

The Small Firms Service for example does not lend money but is possibly the main resource for information on possible sources of finance in your area. They have a database of addresses and contacts both nationally and locally and can put you in touch with the right people in local authorities, government departments, the professions, libraries, chambers of commerce, etc.

For more information look at page 70.

Local councils

Some local councils, especially in city areas, may give grants (money that doesn't have to be repaid) to help small businesses to rent premises and buy equipment. Visit or write to your local council to ask for information about grants.

Trusts and charities

These are organisations which give money for worthy causes. You are only likely to receive a donation if what you are doing is of obvious benefit to the community.

You can obtain a list of all the trusts and charities by looking in the *Directory of Grant Awarding Bodies* (ask at your local library).

Enterprise Allowance Scheme

This is for people receiving unemployment or supplementary benefit and who want to start their own business. Many people in that position hold back because they would normally lose their benefit just at the time when they need it most. The loss of a regular income, even though small, forces them to abandon their plans. The Enterprise Allowance Scheme is designed to overcome this problem.

Fairbridge/YES

The Youth Enterprise Scheme (YES), aimed at assisting young people under 25 to start their own business, has now merged its activities with the Fairbridge Society. For more information look at page 66.

Business proposals

Many bank managers like to see a business proposal or business plan before they give loans. A business proposal should contain:

▷   details about yourself
▷   a description of your product or service
▷   a description of whom you will be selling to (your market), how you know they will buy and how you will advertise
▷   examples of how much you will charge and how you worked out your costings
▷   a **cashflow forecast** of how much you will spend and when you will be receiving money over the next 12 months
▷   an idea of what you will be doing in the future and how you will keep up with any changing trends

The proposal or plan is to show that you have thought about the problems, have done some market research and have a reasonable idea of what you will be able to sell in your first six months or year of business.

Presentation will be important so try to get the proposal typed and put in an attractive folder.

A cashflow forecast

A cashflow forecast is an estimate of **cash out** and **cash in**: how much money you will spend and when you will spend it and how much you will receive and when you expect to get it. It predicts when you are likely to have money and when not. You can use it to plan ahead for times when you have no money to pay for bills or materials.

For example:

In January you have no money left from December. You make £150 (income) and spend £200 (expenditure) so you have a balance of minus £50 (deficit). In February you make £250 and spend £150 so your balance is £100.

This is shown on your forecast like this:

	Cash in	Cash out	Balance
January	£150	£200	(£50)
February	£250	£150	£100

Note – figures in brackets show a minus figure or deficit. So (£50) means −£50.

A full cashflow forecast covers 12 months.

Cashflow forecasts are not just for presenting to banks. Their main purpose is to help you to run your business – to plan ahead and understand where money will come from and what you need to spend it on to run your business.

Find out about the places where you might raise money. Write down the details of what they want from you in return for the loan or grant, including rates of interest. Compare them and decide which might be best if you wanted money to start a business.

1 Brian wants to open a furniture workshop. Write part of a business proposal to present to Brian's bank manager based on the information below:

I want to set up a workshop so I can make and sell furniture. I've already made some pieces and shown them to shops and other potential customers. I have agreements from the following people to buy these things:

The 'Craft Centre' will buy as many rocking chairs and tables as I can produce.

'Wards' will purchase five kitchen tables and twenty chairs in November.

'Smithsons' will purchase one kitchen table and four chairs and re-order every time they are sold.

I charge £50 per rocking chair, £30 per coffee table, £80 per kitchen table and £25 per ordinary chair.

I estimate that, if I had a workshop, it would take three days to make a rocking chair, five days to make eight chairs, two days to make a kitchen table and one and a half days to make a coffee table.

Wood and other materials cost around £10 for a rocking chair, £6 for a coffee table, £15 for a kitchen table and £6 for a chair.

The premises I want will cost £100 per month. I think the electricity bills will be about £45 per quarter on average.

I will need £250 to convert the premises and a further £200 in extra equipment.

For your proposal work out:

▷ how much Brian's raw materials will cost to fulfil his orders for 'Wards' and 'Smithsons'

▷ how long it will take him to make the furniture

▷ how many rocking chairs and coffee tables he will be able to make for the 'Crafts Centre'

▷ how much his materials will cost

The proposal will be dated 1 June. Cover as many points as you can and use the information in this chapter as a guide.

2 Make a simple cashflow forecast for Brian to present to his bank. Remember, it's a prediction of what you think will happen based on what information you have been given. Apart from the definite orders, Brian will be selling to other customers each month. Look carefully at his estimates for the length of time each job takes and try to work out a monthly income for him.

Brian starts trading in July and sells two rocking chairs, three coffee tables, one kitchen table and four chairs. That's cash in. Cash out is his rent, his wood plus a few extras.

Here are the first month's figures:

	Cash in	Cash out	Balance
July	£370	£187	£183

This looks good but remember he has to start making his big order for 'Wards' for which he won't get paid until November. Now continue the forecast for the next 11 months – use your imagination but be realistic.

Now that you have thought about a simple cashflow chart you will have noticed that some months you end up with a positive balance (Brian has made money) and some months you have a negative balance or deficit (Brian has spent more than he's earned).

For example, in a particular month Brian may spend money on wood, tools, rent, transport to move the wood and even on tea and sugar in his workshop. He's been making furniture but not actually selling any. Now Brian can use the money he's made in another month to pay himself and his bills knowing that he will sell his furniture next month.

Brian's cashflow forecast can help him to plan ahead by putting money on one side for months when he will have no money coming in.

Costs

You have already thought about costs when deciding how much to charge (see Chapter 3). Have a quick look at those pages again before continuing.

▷ remember that initial losses are a cost to your business – although you have the money to use you also have to pay it back, so work out regular repayments (usually monthly) as part of your costs

▷ running costs include things like electricity, stationery, stamps and travel, etc.

Materials

The wood he has to buy from the timber suppliers would be Brian's main material cost but he would probably also have to buy screws, nails, wood adhesive and so on. If he expands his range of products he may need to buy things like hinges, locks and handles.

The cost of your materials will vary according to what you make or do. If you make a product you may have to pay a lot of money for materials. You will also have to allow for wastage of materials. For example, if you are dressmaking you may have a lot of odd scraps of material left over. You could cut down on your wastage by using these bits for making something like patchwork cushions or pincushions. In this way the amount of fabric you don't use is cut down so you are making the best use of your materials.

If you are providing a service you will not need to spend so much on materials because the main thing you are selling is your time, work and skills.

A window cleaner's materials are water and window cleaning fluid or soap. The ladder, bucket and cloths are **capital assets**. But if your business involves reselling something you have not made, like fruit and vegetables or cosmetics, then your materials are called **stock**.

Regular bills

Some costs will have to be paid every month or quarter of a year whether you have an income or not. These include the telephone bill, rent, rates, gas electricity and insurance. They are called **fixed overheads**.

Overheads are what your business costs you apart from your materials and your time. They are regular bills that always have to be paid. Fixed overheads stay at much the same price all the time.

Irregular bills

Some bills will vary. For instance sometimes you will pay for publicity – newspaper adverts or posters – but sometimes you won't. Publicity is not a regular bill. Neither is the money you pay for travelling in your business or for stamps, envelopes or writing paper. These are called **variable overheads**.

Capital assets

Variable overheads have to be paid for occasionally during the year but other items you need to pay for only once, or once in a while. These include tools, equipment, machinery and work clothes. They are assets because they are worth money and they are yours. But that's true only if they are useful. Assets have to be kept in good condition and will need repairing and updating from time to time. Include the cost of repairing your capital assets in your cashflow.

Accountants

If you really think that money, cashflow forecasts and other similar money matters are going to be a big problem for you in business you could pay an accountant to work it out for you. You will still have to record all your income and expenditure carefully but they will work it all out for you. An accountant will also be extremely useful when it comes to paying tax. If you don't know how to find an accountant ask other small businesses or people you know if they can recommend one.

Actual cashflow

As you know, a cashflow forecast is only a reasonably good guess at your income and expenditure based on your research. However there may be unexpected costs or your materials could go up in price during the coming year. You may find that you cannot sell as much as you had thought you could.

So during every business year it is a good idea to write down the actual amount of cash out and cash in next to your estimate every month. This will help you to work out if things are going to plan or if you are doing better or worse than you thought. It will also help you to make an even more realistic estimate of the next year's cashflow.

You can do it like this:

	Cash in		Cash out		Balance	
	Forecast	Actual	Forecast	Actual	Forecast	Actual
Month 1	£450	£390	£420	£423	£30	(£33)
Month 2	£320	£330	£210	£215	£110	£115

By doing this you may be able to adjust your cash out by cutting back on things that may not be absolutely necessary. You can keep the balance on the plus side rather than the minus.

 Make a list of different ways you can think of for raising money.

2 Think of your own business idea and make a list of everything you think you will spend money on (expenditure) each month. Here is one person's list that you might like to use as a model:

Expenditure

Stationery	Machinery	Entrance to shows and exhibitions
Telephone bill	Cleaning materials	
Gas and electricity	Work clothes	Trade magazines and papers
Rent and rates	Car/motorbike	
Travel	Postage and packaging	Publicity (ads, leaflets etc.)
Tools	Insurance	

3 Here are lists for a photographer and a gardener. How and why do you think the costs in each business are different? What further costs will each business have?

Photographer	Costs per year	Gardener	Costs per year
Rent	£480	Depreciation of equipment	£40
Rates	£160		
Gas/electricity	£120	Travel (bicycle and repair)	£30
Equipment	£200		
Travel (public transport)	£720	Answerphone	£60
		Advertising	£48
Postage	£240	Stationery	£15
Telephone	£130	Work clothes	£35
Advertising	£240		
Stationery	£50		
Insurance	£30		

4 Here is the beginning of a cashflow chart for a photographer for the first two months of the year. Draw and complete columns for the rest of the year, putting in what you think the photographer could spend and take in each month. Use a pencil at first because you will want to change the figures – you are estimating and won't get it right first time. If you don't know much about photography, choose a product or service you know something about.

CASH FLOW FORECAST

	July	August
Balance at start of month		(£100)
Income		
Customers	£200	£350
Other/loan	£100	–
Total	£300	£350
Expenditure		
Rent	£50	£50
Gas/electricity	£20	–
Materials	£45	£50
Publicity	£20	£20
Insurance	£10	–
Stationery	£25	£5
Postage	£10	£15
Telephone	–	£25
Wages	£100	£100
Equipment	£100	–
Travel	£15	£15
Publications	£5	£5
Total	£400	£285
Balance at end of month	(£100	(35)

5 Imagine that you are a bank manager. Andrew comes to you with a business proposal. He wants to set up a market stall travelling around several markets in nearby towns. He has done quite a bit of market research which convinces you that the costs and amount he will be able to sell are realistic.

Look at his cashflow forecast on the next page. The columns are untotalled. Do you think his business looks possible? Suggest any changes that would improve Andrew's prospects.

Here is Andrew's cashflow forecast:

Cashflow forecast			
	Cash in	Cash out	Balance
January	£ 200	£ 150	£ 50
February	£ 100	£ 100	£ 0
March	£ 100	£ 250	£ (150)
April	£ 250	£ 300	£ (50)
May	£ 500	£ 400	£ 100
June	£ 650	£ 550	£ 100
July	£ 700	£ 450	£ 250
August	£ 600	£ 300	£ 300
September	£ 400	£ 150	£ 250
October	£ 350	£ 350	£ 0
November	£ 450	£ 250	£ 200
December	£ 450	£ 100	£ 350

Progress report

This chapter has given you information about raising the money to start your business. Here are some of the things you have learned:

▷ there are several different ways of raising money and each way has its own advantages and disadvantages

▷ banks and other organisations will want to see a business proposal or plan and a cashflow forecast

▷ a business proposal is a detailed outline of what sort of business you want to start, how you will do it, an estimate of how much it will cost and how much you will make – it will be backed up by a cashflow forecast

▷ a cashflow forecast will detail what you will spend money on and how much money you will get back

▷ when you are in business you should make a note of the actual amount of cash in and cash out so that you can compare it to your forecast – this will enable you to make adjustments as you go along and help you to make a more realistic forecast for the following year

·DISCOVERING·
customers

Martine, aged 22

I like writing and have had some articles published – short stories and different bits and pieces. Magazines, publishers and businesses are my customers. But contacting them and letting them know about me is the hard part. I know they could use my skills and that there are thousands of potential customers. The problem is getting me and them together.

Advertising

There are two main ways of getting customers:

▷   you must go to them
▷   they come to you

Think about different businesses where the customers come to you and those where you go to the customer:

▷   going to the customer – door-to-door salespeople, ice-cream vans, street sellers, sandwich sellers who go round offices and factories
▷   customers coming to you – shops, garages, market stalls

Even the businesses that want the customer to come to them do go out and approach the customer in some way. They persuade the customer to come to them rather than their competitors.

Advertising has one simple message: **Buy from me!**

Advertising puts your product where people see it and tries to persuade them to buy.

Some businesses reach a lot of people on the television. Smaller businesses can advertise in local papers or on local radio.

35

You can see simple advertising in street markets:

It's not such a big step to:

Local papers

Look in your local paper and see how many small businesses advertise there. Notice the different sizes and types of adverts – anything from a couple of lines in the classified advertisements pages, amongst the marriage announcements and cars for sale, to a full-page display with fancy borders, large type and cartoons. Prices vary according to how much space you buy. So, in the classified adverts, a couple of lines with your phone number and what your product or service is might cost you about £5. If you want your advertisements to appear over a long period you might get up to 33% off the price. If you wanted a large space specially set aside for a display advertisement you could well pay hundreds of pounds.

Decide for yourself how much you can afford to set aside for advertising. You may even conclude that local newspapers are not the best place to reach your market and you may decide to try other places. But your chances of reaching your customers through local papers are much higher than if you don't advertise at all.

One person said:

'I discovered that people *did* see my ads, and actually *wanted* to reply to them. But they never actually got around to it. They need reminding again and again and again.'

Local papers often provide additional weekly papers free to every household. These are paid for by advertisers. Rates in them are usually the same as in dailies. Sometimes these free weeklies are operated independently from the main local daily – you'll certainly come across them easily enough.

Word of mouth

Sometimes a small business gets customers because it has done good work or sold a good product. A pleased customer mentions this to a friend and word gets around. This is a very important way in which small businesses become known – it mustn't be underestimated.

It's important that you provide a good, friendly service, but often it can be the little things that lots of businesses forget that make customers remember you. Treat every customer as a potential walking talking advert for your business.

Contacts

Contacts are always important in business. You may not know it yet, but you too have your own network.

Think about how often something similar to this has happened to you:

Ann: I'm looking for a secondhand front wheel for my bike. I can't afford a new one.

Jackie: You know, I think Don has one. He used to have a 175 that he scrapped. You're going to see him on Saturday, aren't you Pete?

Pete: I'll ask him. In fact if he still has it I'll tell him to give you a ring, Ann.

Getting your business known through contacts is almost like doing the same thing in reverse.

It might work like this:

You're making and selling individually designed children's clothes. How many people do you know with children who might be interested? Who do your friends, parents, relatives know? Get them to tell people about your service or product.

Direct selling

If you have a shop or market stall you may think that unless people are interested and come to you there's not a lot you can do.

But there are quite a few ways you get the customers to come to you.

The location of your shop or stall is important (see page 19). You will have already done some market research to find out who your potential customers might be before setting up your business. You probably wouldn't get a lot of customers in a dress shop on an industrial estate. You would need your shop in a shopping area in or near the town centre. And it wouldn't be a good idea to set up a motorbike repair shop in a pedestrian shopping precinct.

You have to persuade customers that your shop or service is better than your competitors. Of course, lower prices and a good service can speak for themselves but you still have to get customers in for the first time. Displays on stalls or in shop windows can make people interested. Try to 'outshine' your competitors by the way things look.

Do it

1 Find out how to put an advert in the local paper. Find out what different types and sizes of adverts there are and how much they cost.

Ask what the circulation (number of papers sold) of one or more of your local papers is. That's roughly how many people would see an advert put in by a local business.

Which local papers have the biggest circulation? How much would it cost to put adverts in them? What sort of advert would be best?

2 Look around your area and make note of the different ways that small businesses advertise.

If you had a limited amount to spend on advertising, say £5 per week, find out what would probably be the most effective way of using it each week.

Could you afford to put a small advert in a bus or an underground train? Find out how much these adverts cost and how long they are displayed for.

3 Don't forget you have to design and print your advert. Think about how you would do this. How much would it cost to have advertisement handouts printed? You could post them door-to-door yourself, give them out in the town centre or put them behind car windscreen wipers.

Have a go at designing an advert for a small business. Design it so that it will make people look at it. Use eyecatching phrases or a simple design and illustrations.

4 Some of the most effective advertising is the most unusual. Think of unusual advertising ideas that would not be very expensive.

Progress report

This chapter is about finding and keeping customers. You have learned:

▷ methods of finding customers
▷ different ways and costs of advertising
▷ a practical way of advertising your business

·DISCOVERING·
how to get started

Paul, aged 25, is a freelance designer

Without being big headed I know I'm a good designer and when I set up on my own I got quite a lot of work. I worked long hours and was raking in the money. I was a bit silly really. I thought all I needed for a good business was to be a good designer. After about six months the problems started. I started getting reminders for bills I thought I'd paid. I didn't know how well I was doing as I'd no proper records. I was doing so well with my design work I'd forgotten about the business side of things; and when it came to sorting out my tax and National Insurance I was completely lost. My thriving business nearly went bust overnight just because I'd neglected the paperwork. I now realise that the paperwork is just as important as being good at what you do.

Organising your records

Paperwork or record-keeping often seems worrying. But compared to the rest it's often the simplest, once you learn how.

Business paperwork means keeping all the receipts and bills you get from suppliers and copies of all the bills and receipts you give to customers. It also means keeping a record of all the exchanges of goods and money that you make in your business.

You do this for several reasons:

▷   to keep a check on how your business is doing
▷   to make sure you know when you have paid your bills and when your customer has paid you
▷   to have accounts ready for when you are assessed for income tax

This is the paperwork you will handle:

Sales invoices

These are bills which state the amount to be paid. You send your customers sales invoices, unless they pay you in cash. It is really a request to be paid for something you have done or supplied.

An invoice looks like this:

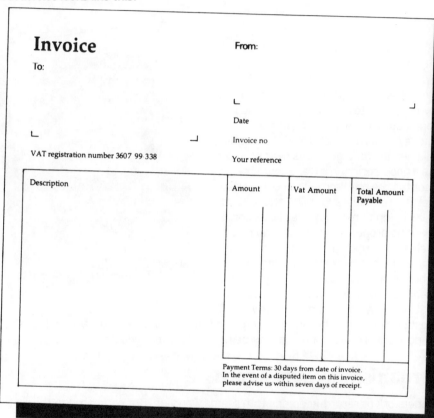

When you send an invoice fill in:

▷ the date
▷ your customer's name and address where it says 'to'
▷ your name and address where it says 'from'
▷ the details of what your customer has bought
▷ the amount your customer must pay

Always keep copies and put them in an **unpaid invoices file**. They are sales invoices because they are your sales. When they are paid, put them in a **paid invoices file**.

40

Receipts

This is the proof that you have paid for something. When you buy from a supplier ask for a receipt, even for very small items like stamps or envelopes. Receipts are proof for the income tax inspector. The tax inspector will accept your receipts as proof of purchase for your business. Many will be **tax deductible**, which means you will not be charged tax on them. You should always give receipts to your customers and keep copies.

A receipt looks like this:

```
                                                      Nº    21

RECEIPT

   DATE _____

   RECEIVED with thanks from
                                    _____
   Name _____
   the sum of        £ _____ in respect of goods & services

   INVOICE NO. _____

   Signed _____
```

When you give a receipt fill in:

▷   the date
▷   the name of the customer where it says 'received from'
▷   the amount paid where it says 'the sum of'
▷   your own signature where it says 'signed'

If each invoice and receipt is numbered it will save you time if you ever have to check back. Most good stationers sell invoice books and receipt books.

Petty cash

Petty cash is money you keep for small things that you need to buy from time to time, like stamps, envelopes, nails, paperclips and so on.

You need a **petty cash box**. You can buy special cash boxes with locks. They are a good idea but you could use any strong tin and keep it in a safe place.

Start with a certain amount in the box, say £10. This is your **float**. Every time you spend some of the money fill in a **petty cash voucher** stating what you bought, when and how much it cost and put it in the box. You can buy special petty cash vouchers but any reasonable note will do.

At the end of every week the amount of money recorded on the petty cash vouchers and the money left in the box should add up to the amount of the original float you had in the box at the start of the week. Write down the amounts spent in a **petty cashbook** making note of what it was spent on and when – get these details from the petty cash vouchers in the petty cash box. Then top up the petty cash box to the original amount again.

In this way you can keep an accurate record of all the money you spend on small items.

Cashbook

Keep detailed records of *all* your transactions in a cashbook. It helps you see at a glance how much cash you have (or don't have). It will also save time and money when your income is assessed by the income tax inspector.

For example:

A photographer has these transactions in one month:

1/7/87 Received £40 from J Smith (customer)
2/7/87 Received £26 from R Toms (customer)
2/7/87 Paid £45 rent
4/7/87 Paid £36 electricity
12/7/87 Received £54 from T Brown (customer)
14/7/87 Paid £20 into petty cash box
14/7/87 Paid £33 for rolls of film
20/7/87 Paid £12 for chemicals
22/7/87 Received £100 grant from council
23/7/87 Paid £98 for camera lens
26/7/87 Paid £12 for photographic paper
27/7/87 Paid £24 for business cards
29/7/87 Received £25 from G White (customer)
30/7/87 Paid £45 to garage for petrol

This is how she wrote the details in her cashbook:

On the left side she entered everything that was paid in, with details of the date paid, who paid and the amount. On the right side she entered everything she had paid for. She included the date she paid it, the person she paid, the item, and the total amount. She also put the amount she paid for specific purposes, like payments to suppliers and for publicity, rent, electricity or travel. This was so that she could see at the end of the month what she spent most of her money on.

If you have been keeping records of all the money you have spent and all the money you have received you can fill in a cashbook sheet like the one opposite for each month.

	Cash in				Cash out	
Date	From	Amount	Date	To		Amount
1/7/87	J Smith	£40·00	2/7/87	RENT: M. Wilberforce		£45·00
2/7/87	R Toms	£26·00	4/7/87	ELECTRICITY: Norweb		£36·00
12/7/87	T Brown	£54·00	14/7/87	PETTY CASH		£20·00
22/7/87	Local Authority Grant	£100·00	14/7/87	PETERSONS PHOTOGRAPHIC: film		£33·00
21/7/87	G White	£25·00	20/7/87	PETERSONS PHOTOGRAPHIC: Developer & fixer		£12·00
			23/7/87	JENNINGS DISCOUNT HI-FI & CAMERA STORE: 35mm lens		£98·00
			26/7/87	PETERSONS PHOTOGRAPHIC: Photo paper		£12·00
			27/7/87	TOWER DESIGN & PRINT: Business Cards		£24·00
			31/7/87	BOROUGHGATE SERVICES: Petrol		£45·00

Total cash in	£245·00	Total cash out	£325·00

£245·00
− £325·00

Balance −£80·00

Sales ledger

This tells you what you have sold to whom, and because sometimes you don't get paid immediately for things that you sell, it's a record of who owes you money.

Every time you sell something you issue a **sales invoice** (see page 40) and fill in the details in your sales ledger. For example:

SALES LEDGER

Date	Details	Price per item	Total	Payment
5/6/87	3 chairs	£25	£75	5/6/87 cash
10/6/87	1 rocking chair	£50	£50	13/6/87 cheque no. 399037244

At the end of the week, or month if you prefer, add up your total sales and cash received. Then make note of anyone who hasn't paid you yet, so that you can send them a reminder letter.

Purchase ledger

This is optional if you keep a cashbook. Use it in the same way as a sales ledger but record things that you have bought in it. These will be larger purchases as opposed to the small purchases recorded in your petty cash book.

It also tells you who you owe money to.

Whom do you need to inform?

Small businesses may not need to inform anyone that they have started until they have been trading for some time. Contact your local Small Firms Service to see if this applies to you. (Find out where they are on page 70.)

These are some places you should contact straight away:

Department of Health and Social Security

Unemployment benefit

If you are self-employed you cannot claim unemployment benefit unless you are doing 'casual' work – not working full-time. To claim you must have worked for long enough previously to have made enough National Insurance contributions to be eligible for unemployment benefit. (This would be roughly eighteen months.)

If you claim unemployment benefit you are allowed to earn up to £2 per day without affecting your benefit. This is after you have deducted your expenses.

Supplementary benefit

Sometimes, if your business is not earning you enough to live on and you work for less than 30 hours per week, you may be able to claim supplementary benefit.

If you claim supplementary benefit you are allowed to earn up to £4 a week without affecting your benefit.

This may seem complicated, but if you are starting a business you may not earn much at first and it's worth going to the DHSS to ask for advice and help. Explain all the facts to them. They will be helpful, especially once they realise you are trying hard to earn your own living.

National Insurance

If you're employed by someone else you have to pay National Insurance. This is deducted from your wage before you get it. Self-employed people also have to pay National Insurance.

44

Employed people pay Class 1 contributions, self-employed people pay Class 2 contributions and Class 4 contributions on profits.

Class 2 is a flat rate contribution of £3.85 (April 1987) per week. But if you earn less than a certain amount you can apply to be let off – get form NI 27A from your Social Security office and you will get a certificate of exemption. Not paying may affect your sickness benefit and your pension so think carefully before claiming exemption.

Class 4 contributions are paid on 6.3% of profits between £4590 and £15340 (April 1987). These contributions are added to your tax.

The Inland Revenue

If you are self-employed you must fill in a tax return at the end of your first year of business. You will be taxed on all the money left over after you have paid your overheads.

You must remember while you are in business to put money aside to save for paying tax at the end of the year. A tax year runs from April to April. You will also have to pay your National Insurance contribution at the same time.

As a rough guide your tax will be about one-third of your profits.

When you start your business, phone or write to your local tax office. You will find the address under Inland Revenue in the phone book. Explain that you have started business. They will start a file for you in which they will keep copies of any correspondence you have with them. They may send you a booklet called *Starting in Business* which explains about tax and related matters.

If you have any tax problems, and especially if you don't understand something, go to the tax office. They are usually very helpful.

Customs and Excise

By law you must register for VAT (Value Added Tax) if your yearly sales are more than £17 000. You can register for VAT before this but you don't have to. Contact the VAT people to find out where you stand. You will find them under Customs and Excise in the phone book.

Companies House

Businesses have to be registered at Companies House – unless you are a **sole trader** or **partnership**. If this is the case, you must display your name and address clearly in your premises. A sole trader is one person and a partnership is two people or more. If your business gets into debt you and your partner, if you have one, are legally responsible for all your debts.

If you form a **limited company** by paying a fee and sending an application to Companies House then legally the business is seen as separate from you personally. You would become a director of the company and you personally would not be strictly liable for the company's debts. Your accounts would be

audited (checked) by an accountant once a year, so you would have to keep proper books.

Write to Companies House for more information. (The address is on page 64.)

If you form a **workers' co-operative** by paying a fee and sending your application to your local Co-operative Development Agency you are also not personally liable for the debts of the company.

Do it

1   John is a carpenter. He starts the week with £10 in his petty cash box.

On Tuesday he needs to buy some nails. He takes £1 out of the box and goes to the shop. The nails cost 87p. When he gets back to his workshop he fills in the voucher for 87p, staples the receipt to it and puts it in his petty cash box.

On Wednesday he needs a pint of milk and a packet of tea. Again he takes £1. They cost 78p. He puts the receipts and a voucher in the box with the 22p change.

On Thursday he breaks a saw blade. A replacement costs exactly £1.20 so he makes out a voucher for that amount, puts it in the box and takes £1.20. When he returns he puts the receipt in the box.

On Friday he needs two new pencils, some envelopes, stamps and a notebook. He takes £3 out of the box. His purchases costs £2.69. When he returns he makes out the voucher for £2.69 and puts it in the box.

Later on Friday he realises that he needs five more 16p stamps. He quickly writes out a voucher for 64p, takes a £1 note and rushes to the post office to catch the last post. When he returns, he throws all the change from his £1 note into the box with a receipt, which he doesn't look at.

On Monday John is filling out his petty cash book. He takes out the vouchers and adds them up. They total £6.18. then he adds up the money in the box. It is £3.22. This comes to £9.40 but the vouchers plus the petty cash in the box should come to £10. John is puzzled so he checks his receipts. One for 87p, one for 78p, one for £1.20 and one for 80p making a total of £3.65. The receipts and the cash add up to £6.87.

John has made several mistakes and as a result his petty cash is very confusing.

Point out John's mistakes by writing up a petty cash book the way it should have been done.

○   What receipts should John have?
○   How much money should have been in the petty cash box first thing on Monday morning?
○   Suggest how he could improve his petty cash procedures so he doesn't make any more mistakes.

46

2 Claire's jewellery business had these transactions in one month:

1/3/87	Paid out £24
2/3/87	Paid for semi-precious stones £42.30
3/3/87	Received for pendant from customer £8.50
3/3/87	Paid for chains £32
3/3/87	Paid for postage £3.20
4/3/87	Paid advance rent for stall at craft fair £15
4/3/87	Paid for advertising £8.60
5/3/87	Received for two rings £9.00
8/3/87	Petrol £13
9/3/87	Jewellery sold at craft fair:
	5 rings £3 each
	1 pendant £7.30
	2 brooches £8 each
	4 chains £4 each
	8 pairs earrings £2.50 each
	3 pairs earrings £5.20 each
	1 ring £13.50
14/3/87	Paid £3 stationery
15/3/87	Received £80 grant from council
18/3/87	Received £7 advance on commission
19/3/87	Paid £30 materials for commission
22/3/87	Paid £25 electricity bill
23/3/87	Received £63 for completed commission piece
24/3/87	Paid advance rent for market stall £10
25/3/87	Received for 1 necklace £12.50
27/3/87	Paid for petrol £7
28/3/87	Jewellery sold on market stall:
	Total £92.35
29/3/87	Received for two necklaces £28.50
29/3/87	Received for one ring £7.20

Draw up and fill in Claire's cashbook correctly.

Progress report

This chapter covers some basics about starting up. You have learned:

▷   the organisations you need to contact when starting up
▷   what business records you need to keep
▷   how to keep petty cash and a cashbook
▷   how your National Insurance payments will be affected by your business

·DISCOVERING·
what next

Esmail, aged 21

I set up my own removal and light haulage business. After about two years I'd managed to pay off my original loan to my father and built up a small group of regular customers. Things seemed to be going well and I'd managed to save some money. I've got to admit I'd been working for about 70 to 80 hours a week, every week, and living on practically nothing. After a lot of thought I bought another van and took on my first employee. I don't make a lot more money because of it, but I can offer a better service and I'm only working for about 65 hours a week now.

Susan, aged 20

Two years ago I set up a mobile disco. I borrowed £300 from my parents and got a bank loan of £250 using my disco console as collateral to guarantee the loan. I'd saved up for about a year to buy that. After about four months things were going great. I was taking about £80 each week. I decided to buy an old van on hire purchase and invested in a smoke machine and strobe lights. I always made sure I had the latest records as that kept my disco popular.

As the months went by, takings crept up to about £120 a week. I thought that if I set up another disco I could double the amount. I'd do the gigs further away in the van and pay someone about £50 a week to do the local ones. A secondhand console cost

48

£140 but I didn't need to spend that much more on records as we could rotate them between the two mobiles.

The next few months were a disaster. Instead of doubling the takings we were using the two mobile discos to do only about two extra gigs a week. I was only taking about £50 each week on the other disco and that was more than swallowed up by the wage and expenses. All my reserve money was being used up to run an extra disco – I was losing money. I had to sell off the new equipment and some other things just to stop myself getting into debt. I'd tried to grow too fast. Now I'm taking things steadily, and building up ever so slowly. I'm thankful I've still got my disco.

Many established businesses have problems keeping going. Yours could be no exception. What do you need to think about once you've started?

Help in running the business

Don't expect things always to run smoothly or the business to grow steadily. You will run into problems – every business does!

It will always be up to you to solve your problems and make final decisions because it's your business. You probably wouldn't want it any other way. But there are lots of ways of getting help and advice.

Here are some of them:

Friends, relatives and other businesses

You may have got help from friends or relatives when you started your business. They may be willing to help you or give you advice. They may be well-meaning but, unless they really have similar experience, their advice may not be totally reliable. So it may be all right to ask them for advice about small problems, but for big problems or technical problems get advice from experienced professionals.

There are three kinds of professionals you can go to and whose business is money:

▷   bank managers
▷   solicitors
▷   accountants

Bank managers

Your bank can give you business advice. This is especially true if they have lent you any money. They want your business to do well so they will have their loan repaid and they will hope that you will bank with them when your business goes well. Don't be afraid to go to your bank for advice – they really will be able to give you professional help. Some banks even have special sections for helping businesses.

Accountants and solicitors

You don't have to use them all the time – just when it suits you. Accountants and solicitors will charge according to what they actually do, so you can keep your costs down by asking them to do the tasks you know you cannot do yourself. Later on, you will probably be able to make up your own books and accounts by looking closely at the work they have done for you and learning from it.

Initially, though, accountants and solicitors are probably indispensable, and they will pay for themselves in terms of freedom from worry. But you can't escape the fact that they are expensive so include likely costs in your budget. You can sort out well in advance who you will eventually use by asking around for recommendations and comparing their costs. You can ask them the right questions too. For example, instead of asking 'What do you charge?' you can ask 'On what basis do you charge?' You are then more likely to get the kinds of details you need to make accurate comparisons.

If you feel you can't afford an accountant or solicitor, consider them as people who can actually save you money in the long run. You could spread the cost of using one over a year and just use them for the essentials. Putting money aside for essentials is good business practice.

In the long run, it will pay you to learn to manage your own books and accounts. It's not difficult – if you have the gumption to go it alone, then you certainly have the gumption to learn a few new skills with figures. If you can manage household accounts – money in and bills out etc. – you can certainly manage small business accounts. It's just the same principles applied to something a little more complicated.

Local agencies

Throughout the country there are organisations and schemes to help and encourage small businesses. They may be run by local councils, chambers of commerce, government departments, big industries etc. Most libraries will have information about local schemes and addresses of local branches of national schemes.

You can get advice from the Small Firms Service, Local Enterprise Agencies, and other bodies. Talk it through with someone who knows. The Small Firms Service offers free advice for the first three sessions. The fourth session onwards is chargeable (at present £30 + VAT) but in practice most people's problems are sorted out well before then.

This is only a small indication of some of the people who can help you. Look at the list of useful addresses and also look at the booklist on page 63. It's your business but you need never be stuck for help.

Growth

When you've set up your business you want it to survive and perhaps make it grow. But one of the biggest mistakes small businesses make is to expand too fast. The experiences of Esmail and Susan illustrate this. Esmail worked hard to get his business established once he had set up. He only tried to expand once he had paid off his original debts and put some of his profits aside. Also, he didn't try to live too extravagantly at the start.

Susan expanded her business too quickly and only just escaped getting into serious debt. She spent money, assuming that doubling the size of her business would mean doubling her income. If Susan had done her market research she would probably have known there was enough business for one disco in the area but not two. Her cashflow and planning could have told her very quickly that she was heading for trouble.

Growing can mean needing to buy more materials or take on staff to do the added work, so you commit your spending before the money comes in. What would happen if the work was just a one-off or not suitable for your business for other reasons?

Employees

The time may come when your business grows and you need staff to help with the work.

You will need to consider several things:

o   Will the extra work you get from employing someone be worth paying their wage?
o   If you employ someone you become an employer and you take on new responsibilities (tax, National Insurance, sick pay and the responsibilities outlined in the Health and Safety at Work Act).
o   Would a part-time worker be enough?

Here is a brief outline of what you need to know if you become an employer:

Tax

You will be responsible for deducting tax from your employees' wages to pass on to the Inland Revenue under the Pay As You Earn (PAYE) Scheme. You can find out about this from the Inland Revenue.

National Insurance

You have to make a contribution to the DHSS for your employees as well as their contribution. The Department of Health and Social Security issue a leaflet, NP15 *Employers Guide to National Insurance Contributions*, telling you about this.

Sick pay

Employers pay basic sick pay for the first eight weeks that an employee is ill. They can reclaim the money through PAYE.

Health and safety at work

The Health and Safety at Work Act says employers have responsibilities to safeguard employees and others at work. This includes times when workers are outside premises, for example a van driver. You *must* insure yourself against employees having accidents because they might sue you. This is called **employers' liability insurance** and is a legal necessity if you employ someone.

It means that if an employee suffers personal injury or disease arising out of, or in the course of, their employment in Great Britain, any compensation will be paid by the insurance company. Employers have to insure employees to cover at least £2 million arising out of any one claim. That doesn't mean of course that as an employer you have to find £2 million of your own, but it does mean you are responsible for making sure that the premiums you pay to the insurance company are enough to provide the cover you need to protect your employees.

In one case fairly recently, a transport firm covered themselves with £5 million for damage to other property. One of their lorries ran into a motorway bridge and caused £20 million of damage. Their insurance company paid the £5 million they were covered for, but the firm had to find another £15 million difference.

To find a company that gives employers' liability insurance, go to an insurance broker or insurance consultant that specialises in your kind of business, look at the Yellow Pages and ask around your colleagues, friends, or people in other businesses for their recommendations.

If you want to look more closely at the Health and Safety at Work Act, your local library will have a copy, or will be able to get one. It is also available through your local bookshop, though you may have to order it specially. The nearest office of the Health and Safety Executive will have a copy. The environmental health department of local authorities is responsible for enforcing the Act in offices and shops. Ask at your local council offices and look at page 73 for the addresses of health and safety consultants.

Bankruptcy

This can happen to any business. Basically, bankruptcy is what happens when your debts are more than your assets (what the company owes and is owed). An individual goes **bankrupt**. A company goes into **liquidation**. The two things mean the same.

Voluntary liquidation

If your debts are getting out of hand and you think you can't manage you can go into liquidation. That means that you decide you will no longer be trading after a certain date. It's a decision you take by yourself, for yourself. Just how easy or difficult the process of winding up your business is depends very much on how complicated it is. If you are in something simple like window-cleaning, then it will be easy enough, you just sell your equipment – ladders etc. – and don't clean any more windows. If you are making something, like craft goods, it might be more complicated if for example you have outstanding orders from customers who have paid for their goods already. If you don't have the cash to repay them, then it could get messy.

Bankruptcy

Bankruptcy is a harder way of finishing. It means essentially that your financial and business affairs are taken out of your hands and looked after by the Official Receiver. If you ever get to the stage when you know that bankruptcy is absolutely the only thing left to do, you have to file a petition of bankruptcy. You will need the help of a solicitor, who will charge you. If you have no money anyway, and are already in debt, you certainly don't want this. But if it does happen, the Official Receiver will handle all your affairs and arrange to pay off your creditors. It may take up to five years to discharge your status as bankrupt, so it really is a drastic last resort.

Much better therefore never to let yourself get that far down. It's much worse than being unemployed!

So, before you go it alone, be absolutely sure that it's what you want to do. Many people go into self-employment as a way off the dole. There is absolutely nothing wrong with that, but it's only fair to point out that many people last only a short time on their own. And if you do have to finish, it's much better to keep as much control over your life as you can by going into voluntary liquidation before things get too bad.

You always have the support of the Small Firms Service. Staying in contact with the people who know, and who can guide you, is good business practice. It's good psychology too – there's nothing worse than feeling there's absolutely nobody to share your burdens with. Everybody *wants* you to succeed.

Planning

It's not only when setting up a business that you need to plan – you need to keep planning to keep your business going and to expand.

You need to keep developing your management skills. Don't worry if your management skills aren't up to scratch when you start. You'll learn.

Sometimes it's a case of knowing when to find things out and who to go to for advice – you'll learn about that too.

How to assess your management skills

Running a business needs some management skills. Management means planning, organising and being able to learn from people or from mistakes. It also means doing the paperwork and other routine tasks. Lots of people who start businesses think they haven't got management skills but are surprised to realise, after a while, that they have.

This list names some of the skills you may need in managing a business:

Management skills

Finding things out
Designing and improving things
Selling
Giving information
Describing things
Working with figures
Getting money people owe you

Making things/putting plans into operation

Technical details of your product or service
Buying supplies
Planning your work
Checking your work

People/organisations

Selecting and asking people to help
Working with people
Giving instructions
Persuading people
Listening to people

Finance/paperwork

Raising money
Looking for premises
Managing money
Keeping records
Book-keeping
Tax and insurance
Writing letters

Copy out the list of skills above. On the right hand side of the page make five columns headed **good**, **fair**, **know someone who can help**, **weak**, **don't know**. Put a tick in one of these columns next to each of the skills listed. Check your score on page 62.

Of course you probably haven't ever run a business of your own so think of things you have done while you work down the list.

For example:

On the list of management skills, one item is 'technical details of your produce or service'. This is really about understanding and being able to explain the details of your product or service. Think about whether you have ever described or discussed a film or television programme that particularly interested you, or talked about the design of a piece of clothing or even a recipe.

Remember, this is not a test. Be honest with yourself!

Management skills

The rest of this chapter looks at each of the points in the management skills questionnaire. It sets some tasks for practice and it points out some places where you can get help from.

Finding things out

Libraries are a good source of information. If you aren't sure how to use library indexing systems go to your nearest library and ask the librarian or library assistant how to use them. Many libraries have **microfiche** indexes. The index is printed on film cards and viewed with a small screen. Ask how to use this.

 Find a specific book. Perhaps you could try to find one of those listed on page 63.

Did you know that you can get almost any book you want from any library through their inter-library loan scheme? This means that the library borrows the book for you from another library. Ask your library about it.

 Look round the reference section – you'll be surprised at how much information even small libraries have that can help you with a small business. Practise using the library and at the same time find out more about aspects of business covered in this chapter.

Find out about:

▷ PAYE
▷ National Insurance
▷ The Health and Safety at Work Act

 Make a note of the publications and books you got information from so that you can find them easily in the future.

Designing and improving things

Have you ever altered something to improve it, for example a recipe, a mechanical part, a model, a bike or an electrical item?

Have you ever thought of a simple solution to a problem by designing something? Think of several simple household items, for example a lampshade, a can opener or a corkscrew. Discuss ways in which you might be able to improve or re-design them.

Remember, if you have an idea for a simple item that is new, and which you might be able to sell, you might want to get it patented so that no one can steal your idea.

Contact the Patents Office or the Design Council for help with design ideas.

Selling

Some people have the knack of selling things. Usually it needs an outgoing, confident personality. You may be good at making things but not a natural seller. You still have to sell yourself or your product.

What if you think you're no good at selling? You will gain confidence with experience.

1 When you're out shopping notice how sales people in shops behave. Do they make you feel relaxed, or do they annoy you?

   Learn from the good things they do and from their mistakes.

2 Notice which adverts have an effect on you. What sort of styles make you notice them?

3 What sort of selling gimmicks have most impact?
   Can you think of any selling gimmicks that you could use?
   Think about how presentation and packaging affect the customer.
   After all, two identical products may sell differently because one is packaged nicely and the other in a plain box.

4 Remember – there are laws about selling.

   Find out about:

▷ The British Code of Advertising Practice
▷ The Trades Descriptions Act (1968)

You will be able to get help and advice from the Institute of Practitioners in Advertising and the Advertising Standards Authority.

Giving information and describing things

Here are some ideas for practising this:

1 Find the manual for a piece of machinery, an electrical item or similar. Re-write it in your own words.

2 By drawing a diagram with accompanying explanation, show someone in detail how to:

o   use a stereo or hi-fi
o   operate a sewing maching
o   use an electric food mixer
o   use an electric typewriter or micro-computer

The best way to test if you have explained things well is to ask your 'trainee' to do what you have explained, if they couldn't do it before you started.

Working with figures

Running your own business will usually involve some number work. Some businesses don't need much more than basic maths and a logical, orderly ability. A calculator will be of great help.

If you need some help with your maths most colleges run maths courses as evening classes. Many unemployment centres and drop in centres have courses that you can attend on a casual basis. Find out if there's one near you (check at colleges or your local library).

Getting money people owe you

Any business, sooner or later, comes across a customer who doesn't pay up.

1 You can get advice from a solicitor or your local Citizens' Advice Bureau (look them up in your telephone directory).
You will get advice from them free of charge and you may get a certain amount of free advice from a solicitor under the Legal Aid Scheme.

2 Find out the simplest legal procedure to make a customer who owes you money pay up.

Buying supplies

Think of your business idea and what supplies you will need.

1 Make a list of supplies.

2 Find out two places where you could buy supplies.
Which place is cheapest? List the advantages and disadvantages of each supplier. Consider the quality of materials, distance, service, the range of choice, and so on.

Planning your work

1 Plan the journey in detail and write down your plan.

Now find out:
- which bus and/or train to catch?
- where to catch it/them?
- when and where will they arrive?
- approximately when will you get to your destination?
- how will you return home?
- what is the exact price?

If it is not the cheapest way, say why your travel methods are necessary.

2 Think of the average day's work that you do. How could you plan your time and the order of your tasks to give yourself more time for other things you want to do?

Checking your work

1 At the end of each task or day's work, do you have any system by which you check that you have done everything correctly? If so, what is it? Does it work? If not, how could you invent a checking system?

2 Cashflow charts can help you to plan and to keep a check on your business. Your cashflow forecast is like a plan and helps you keep a check on the actual cashflow. This is a simple cashflow forecast. In the column marked 'actual' are the figures for what really happened. The balance (right hand columns) has not been filled in.

Cashflow forecast

	Cash in		Cash out		Balance	
	Forecast	Actual	Forecast	Actual	Forecast	Actual
September	£150	£124.75	£350	£350.00		
October	£200	£134.80	£300	£385.47		
November	£250	£209.12	£300	£320.46		
December	£300	£244.84	£570	£525.50		
January	£400	£381.70	£400	£410.95		
February	£750	£824.35	£300	£244.55		
March	£800	£767.42	£375	£249.40		
April	£800	£781.45	£570	£534.70		
May	£750	£903.94	£375	£291.83		
June	£750	£732.39	£360	£286.44		
July	£650	£720.18	£520	£546.74		
August	£550	£604.26	£600	£584.20		

Work out the figures yourself and see what the difference is between the forecast and the actual performance. (If you need help to remember about cashflow forecasts look at pages 28–32.)

o   Did the business make a profit over the year?
o   How was the business planning more as it went on? Suggest why business seems to improve as time goes on.
o   Is there a tendency to spend more than the forecast and to receive less than the forecast?
o   Can you suggest ways this business could improve its performance?
o   How well or how badly do you think the projected figures were done?

Selecting and asking people to help

 1 Who would you go to for help with these problems?

o   You need to buy new machinery to speed up your production. You can't afford to buy it but you know it would pay for itself in about one year. The machine would cost £350.
o   You don't understand about your National Insurance payments.
o   You have to submit your income tax returns but you are having problems sorting out your accounts.
o   You want to start a small advertising campaign locally for a new range of products you are making and selling.

 2 At some time you may need to employ someone. You will probably have to interview a few people.

This is an exercise for you to practise interviewing people and deciding which person would be best for your purpose.

Think of your business idea and why you might need an employee. Work out exactly what you would want the employee to do and write out a brief job description.

Get a group of people to act as applicants for the job. Give them each a copy of the job description. Interview each of them in turn and decide which one you would employ and why. It will be good interview practice for them also.

Discuss the whole exercise as a group afterwards.

Working with people

Think of different occasions when you have worked with other people.
Can you get on with people you don't know very well?
Do you feel relaxed with strangers?
Are you able to talk to people you've just met or do you get shy or quiet?
Talk about these things with others.

Giving instructions and persuading people

There are good and bad ways to give instructions and persuade people to do things.

Discuss these problems as a group:

1 You take on someone to help out in the shop. She is about twice your age. She is generally a very good worker but she has made a mistake. Tell her she has made a mistake and how to correct it without offending her. She is a very sensitive person.

2 You employ a signwriter to make an advertising board to go outside your shop. You have very precise ideas for what it should look like (think of a design for one). Write down instructions for the signwriter to follow while working on the advertising board.

3 How will you persuade someone who is interested in what you produce that it is better than the competition?

Try acting out the situation with one person as the potential customer and one as the 'persuader'. Remember, different people require different methods of persuasion. Try acting out the situation with different people.

Listening

1 Get a friend to read out a long paragraph or a page from a book or magazine while you listen. Afterwards they can ask you questions about the passage they have read to check how carefully you listened and what you can remember.

2 Listen to and watch the news on television. Afterwards write down all the details of a major news item that you can remember. If you want to check on how accurate you were you could try to get another person to watch with you and then compare notes.

Raising money

1 List the different ways of raising money for starting a business. Check by looking on pages 26–27 and asking people.

2 Which method of raising finance do you think would be most suitable for *you* if you were setting up a business?

Premises

1 List the different ways to find premises suitable for a business idea you have.

2 Using the methods that you have listed look around your area for business premises that would be suitable for your business idea.

Try to find out who owns each property, or is renting it, how much it is and so on.

Build up a file of premises over a period of one or two weeks. (For help look at pages 20–21.)

Managing money and keeping records

1 Keep a record of your own money for about three months. Do it as if you are a business by preparing a cashflow for three months.

2 Also make your own cashbook and fill it in under the sections cash in and cash out.

Do you get more efficient at managing and accounting for your money as time goes on?

Book-keeping

Do you keep any sort of records, for example records of spending, savings, scores or mileage?
Do you make lists, for example shopping lists or lists of things to do?

Any of these things may indicate that you would manage book-keeping for business without too much difficulty because you are an orderly person. Book-keeping is just a matter of keeping records and being orderly.

Talk about this and decide how much you rate it for managing a business.

Tax and insurance

Talk about these things to find out exactly what they are and how they affect your business. If you don't know, find out.

▷ National Insurance
▷ different class of National Insurance payments and what they mean
▷ VAT
▷ a tax year
▷ tax deductable
▷ PAYE
▷ employers' liability insurance

Writing business letters

Business letters need to be simple and clear. They need to give the message you want to give, without frills or decoration. That doesn't mean they have to be unfriendly – far from it. All you have to do is say what you want to say, or ask for the thing you want, in a plain and easy way.

There are generally accepted ways of laying out letters which make it easy for people to pick out the information they want.

There is much useful information and clear advice in *Letter Writing*, by Ruth Lesirge and Roz Ivanic. Look also at *Improve Your Writing*, and *Communications Themes and Skills*.

Results

Good

If most of your ticks were in the **good** column, you evidently feel confident with yourself that you have the management skills needed to run your own business. You are well organised, good at planning and looking ahead, and happy working with both people and things. No problems anywhere – you will do fine.

Fair

If most of your ticks were in the **fair** column, you won't have any difficulties either. In some respects you may well be in a better position than if you had most ticks in the good column, because you are not overconfident. Your caution will stand you in good stead.

Know someone who can help

If most were in the **know someone who can help** column, you are in a very sound position indeed. You know the things you need help with and you know where to get help. What could be better? The way forward is easy. Make contact with your source of help on the things you're not sure of – having support and encouragement takes away a lot of anxieties.

Weak

If most were in the **weak** column, you're honest with yourself, but check anyway that you're not being too hard on yourself. If you genuinely are weak in most areas, there's no better way to improve your skills that talking with people who know the subject and reading about it.

This book is a excellent first step. Use it to the full. Look up all the contacts, addresses and telephone numbers it gives. Don't just read the 'Do it' sections – have a go at them. Get support from the organisations listed and from your friends and relations. All you need is the confidence!

Don't know

If you ticked **don't know** most, it seems you are not confident about your abilities at all. Setting up in business needs determination and even courage – there can be a lot at stake. Maybe it's not for you at all. But don't despair – why not team up with other people? Then you can let the skills that you know you have really shine, and get support from the others too. If you really want to go it alone you have a lot of homework to do! You're definitely in the right place with this book.

How did you score yourself?

more to read

More to read

Here is a brief selection of books and leaflets. Find them, together with many others, at your local library.

Action for Jobs: Opening More Doors, (Department of Employment)
   This describes the employment, training and enterprise programmes offered by the government. It is available free through Jobcentres.

The Small Business Kit, (National Extension College)

Be Your Own Boss, (National Federation of Self-employed and Small Businesses Ltd)

The Guardian Guide to Running a Small Business, (Kogan Page)

Daily Telegraph Guide to Self-employment, (Kogan Page)

Your Own Business, (BBC Publications)

Work for Yourself, (National Extension College)

All Our Own Work, Co-operating for Work and *Down to Business*, (COIC)

Letter Writing, Ruth Lesirge and Roz Ivanic, (Macmillan Education)

Improve Your Writing and *Improve Your Number Skills*, (Longman/COIC)
   Available from the Resources Unit, 62 Hallfield Road, Layerthorpe, York YO3 7XQ, tel.: (0904) 425444

Communication Themes and Skills, (COIC)

Second Chances for Adults, (COIC)

The Open Learning Directory, (UNESCO)

If you have got this far and done some of the things this book suggests . . .

If you have looked at each section and read the stories of the young business people in them . . .

If you have found yourself nodding in agreement or violently disagreeing because of your own experience . . .

If you have experienced some of the joys and problems described in this book . . .

Then . . . You have discovered business. Use your discovery because now we're in business!

Here are the addresses mentioned in the book and some other useful contact points.

Business in the Community

227a City Road
London EC1B 1LX
Tel.: (01) 253 3716

Provides information and addresses of all local enterprise agencies.

Careers Service

Local careers services provide advice on training and employment opportunities, particularly for younger people. The address of your local careers office is in the phone book under the local education authority or careers service.

Companies House

Crown Way
Maindy
Cardiff CF4 3UZ
Tel.: (0222) 388588

Provides information on how to set up a limited company.

Co-operative Development Agency

Broadmead House
21 Panton Street
London SW1Y 4DR
Tel.: (01) 839 2988

Advises, promotes, represents and carries out research into worker co-operatives.

Council for Small Industries in Rural Areas (CoSIRA)

141 Castle Street
Salisbury
Wiltshire SP1 3TP
Tel.: (0722) 336255

Gives advice to small firms in rural areas. They can also provide financial assistance for businesses to set up.

The Crafts Council Administration Offices

12 Waterloo Place
London SW1Y 4AU
Tel.: (01) 930 4811

Helps people in crafts businesses with information and advice. Can help with marketing and even provide grants.

Department of Trade and Industry/
Industry Department for Scotland

1 Victoria Street
London SW1H 0ET
Tel.: (01) 215 7877

Alhambra House
45 Waterloo Street
Glasgow G2 6AT
Tel.: (041) 248 2855

Assistance for businesses is also available through a number of schemes administered by DTI and IDS.

Employment Measures Units

These offices will be pleased to give you advice and information on the New Workers Scheme, the Job Release Scheme and the Job Splitting Scheme:

Midlands
2 Duchess Place
Hagley Road
Birmingham B16 8NS
Tel.: (021) 456 1144

North West
Sunley Building
Piccadilly Plaza
Manchester M60 7JS
Tel.: (061) 832 9111

North East
Condercum House
171 West Road
Newcastle upon Tyne NE15 6PL
Tel.: (091) 272 2294

South East
Telford House
Hamilton Close
Basingstoke
Tel.: (0256) 29266

Wales and South West
1st Floor, Block 4
Government Buildings
St Agnes Road
Cardiff CF4 3UF
Tel.: (0222) 693131

Scotland
Pentland House
47 Robb's Loan
Edinburgh EH14 1UE
Tel.: (031) 443 8731

Enterprise Allowance Scheme

Find out about this from your local Jobcentre.

It pays you up to £40 a week to compensate for loss of benefit and to help you get established. But there are a number of conditions:

▷   you must be receiving unemployment or supplementary benefit

▷   you must have been unemployed for at least 13 weeks when you apply

▷   you must be able to show you have at least £1000 available which you are prepared to invest in the business in the first 12 months (it can be in the form of a loan or overdraft, and the scheme can give advice on other ways of raising the money)

▷   you must not have received the allowance for another previous business

▷   it must be approved by the Manpower Services Commission

The allowance is payable only for 52 weeks.

Enterprise and Deregulation Unit

Suggestions for deregulation should be sent to:

Department of Employment
Caxton House
London SW1H 9NF

Fairbridge/YES (Youth Enterprise Scheme)

Victoria Chambers
16–20 Strutton Ground
London SW1P 2HP
Tel.: (01) 222 3341

The Youth Enterprise Scheme (YES) was an initiative by the National Association of Youth Clubs. The scheme has two objectives:

1   To provide small sums of capital not normally exceeding £5000 to enable young people under the age of 25, who in most cases will have been unemployed for three months, to set up in business, either as sole traders, as partnerships or as a company/co-operative.

2   To provide help and advice to enable them to do so with reasonable expectation of success.

The scheme provides awards of up to £250 to enable applicants for YES loans to 'test the market', up to £75 for 4 sessions at a local open air market or car boot sale etc., and (sponsored by Barclays Bank) £250 to assist in the purchase of cars or vans where these are a fundamental part of the business. There are also grants toward the cost of courses.

The merger with Fairbridge enables the scheme to expand further since the combined assets of the two charities now amount to just over £6 million. The new organization is called Fairbridge/YES.

Practical Action (at the same address) tries to find equipment for young people's projects.

Highlands and Islands Development Board

Bridge House
27 Bank Street
Inverness IV1 1QR
Tel.: (0463) 234171

Instant Muscle

PO Box 48
Farnham
Surrey
Tel.: (06286) 63926

Provides help with feasibility studies and business plans, as well as hand-holding for 18 to 30-year-olds.

Livewire

National Extension College
18 Brooklands Avenue
Cambridge CB2 2HN
Tel.: (0223) 316644

Provides free advice to 16 to 25-year-olds with promising business ideas(including co-operatives).

Local Enterprise Agencies

Local Enterprise Agencies can offer a wide range of advice and support to small businesses and those setting up in business. For your nearest agency, contact:

Business in the Community
Tel.: (01) 253 3716

Scottish Business in the Community
Tel.: (031) 556 9761

The Local Enterprise Development Unit

Ledu House
Upper Balwally
Belfast BT8 4TB
Tel.: (0232) 691031 or Freephone 7722

Provides information and advice for small businesses in Northern Ireland.

Manpower Services Commission

A number of government training schemes are run through the MSC. Contact them through your nearest regional office of the MSC training division:

London (01) 278 0363
Midlands (021) 643 6338
Northern (0632) 326181
North-west (061) 833 0251
Scotland (031) 225 8500

South-east (0256) 29266
South-west (0272) 273710
Wales (0222) 388588
Yorkshire and Humberside
(0532) 446299

National Association of Youth Clubs

30 Peacock Lane
Leicester
Tel.: (0533) 29514

National Youth Bureau

17–23 Albion Street
Leicester LE1 6GD
Tel.: (0533) 554775

Helps with advice on training, publishes a booklet containing case studies and provides information (including the national award scheme sponsored by Shell UK).

New Workers Scheme

Contact the nearest Employment Measures Unit regional office, New Workers Scheme section.

Employers can claim £15 per week for employees who:

▷ are under 21
▷ are within their first year of employment
▷ have exhausted YTS entitlement
▷ are unable to find a suitable YTS continuation place

68

Jobs offered must:

▷ be expected to last at least 52 weeks
▷ have an average 35 paid hours a week
▷ pay a gross weekly wage of not more than £55 for those under 20 and £60 for 20-year-olds (payments are made quarterly in arrears, for a maximum claim period of 52 weeks per individual)

Project Full Employ

102 Park Village East
London NW1 3FP
Tel.: (01) 387 1222

Runs courses on self-employment.

Race Relations Employment Advisory Service

London (SE and SW England)
Tel.: (01) 839 5600 ext. 2244

Birmingham (West Midlands and Wales)
Tel.: (021) 643 8191 ext. 2891

Nottingham (East Midlands)
Tel.: (0602) 413401/581224

Leeds (Yorkshire and Humberside, Northern Region)
Tel.: (0532) 438232

Manchester (NW and Scotland)
Tel.: (061) 832 9111 ext. 2226

Royal Jubilee Trusts

8 Bedford Row
London WC1R 4BA
Tel.: (01) 430 0524

Provides details of resources and help available for young people's projects – not usually business orientated.

Scottish Development Agency

120 Bothwell Street
Glasgow G2 7JP
Tel.: (041) 248 2700

People aged 16 to 25 who wish to set up their own businesses in Glasgow, Bathgate, Inverclyde or Ardrossan, Stevenston or Saltcoats may be eligible for assistance from the Enterprise Funds for Youth (EFFY) scheme funded by the SDA and administered on a pilot basis by local enterprise trusts. Under the scheme, low-interest loans of up to £3000 may be awarded to young people with viable business propositions.

The SDA, with financial assistance from the European Social Fund, also sponsors the Training and Employment Grants Scheme (TEGS) in special project areas (Leith, Dundee, Coatbridge, Motherwell, Clydebank and Glasgow Eastern Area Renewal) and other selected areas where the Agency is assisting local employment initiatives. TEGS helps employers to recruit and train local people. It is specifically aimed at unemployed people between 17 and 24 and those of 25 and over who have been out of work for a minimum of 12 months.

Scottish Enterprise Foundation

Stirling University
Stirling FK9 4LA
Scotland
Tel.: (0786) 73171 ext. 2171

Small Firms Service

Tel.: Freephone Enterprise 2444

Broadly, they offer two services: the information service, which is free, and the counselling service, of which the first three sessions are free. There are over 100 area counselling officers and 13 Small Firms Centres nationally, so you need not travel far. They will provide information and leaflets giving advice.

If for example you want to know about tax incentives to expand, the Small Firms Service can tell you about the Business Expansion Scheme. This is organised by the Inland Revenue, and with it you can get up to £40000 tax relief to invest in other businesses.

In Scotland the service is operated through the Scottish Development Agency. In Wales the information service is provided by The Welsh Office and the counselling service is operated by the Welsh Development Agency.

Small Firms Information Service – Scotland

Roseberry House
Haymarket Terrace
Edinburgh EH12 5EZ
Tel.: (031) 337 9595

Provides an information service to small firms and firms being set up.

Unemployment Benefit Offices

The staff are always ready to advise you about the unemployment benefit you might be entitled to.

Welsh Development Agency

Pearl Building
Greyfriars Road
Cardiff CF1 3XX
Tel.: (0222) 32955/222666

Small Business Unit

Treforest Industrial Estate
Pontypridd
Mid Glamorgan CF37 5UT
Tel.: (044) 385 2666/385 3021

Provides advice for small businesses in Wales.

Young Entrepreneurs Fund

The Seymour Suite
65/69 Walton Road
East Molesey
Surrey KT8 0DP
Tel.: (01) 783 1099

The Young Entrepreneurs Fund was set up to help young people aged 20 to 40 to build and develop successful businesses.

A fund of £1 million has been established which will be used to make equity investments (normally of between £50000 and £100000) in suitable companies. Some of the fund will also be used for smaller businesses and start-ups. A financial advisor and a panel of experts will also be available for the businesses concerned.

One of the main areas of interest to the Fund is 'Young Entrepreneurs Business'. Criteria to be applied are:
▷   good market potential
▷   determined and motivated applicants
▷   ability to produce regular performance reports for the purpose of monitoring progress.

Any profits realised by the Fund will be reinvested in other young entrepreneurs and their companies.

Young Enterprise

Robert Hyde House
48 Bryanston Square
London W1H 7LN
Tel.: (01) 724 7641

Offer a part-time simulation exercise over 9 months for 15 to 19-year-olds. Principally involved in helping to implement business projects, they usually work with groups of students rather than individuals and often operate within schools and colleges to provide practical experience.

Youth Business Initiative

Prince's Trust
8 Bedford Row
London WC1R 4BU
Tel.: (01) 430 0524

This is part of the Prince's Trust/Royal Jubilee Trust. It provides limited bursaries not exceeding £1000 for each recipient and up to a maximum of £3000 for a partnership of three.

Basic conditions are that it is available for unemployed people between 18 and 25 years old considering self-employment as an option. Applicants should be British subjects. Bursaries are aimed at assisting in the early stages of establishment of small businesses which will lead to permanent self-employment. The finance available is not for use as working capital but for the purchase of tools, equipment, transport, and payment of insurance, professional fees or further training. It is essential that the bursaries are supplemented by an educational/training element provided by experienced adults.

Design

The Design Council

28 The Haymarket
London SW1Y 4SU
Tel.: (01) 839 8000

May be able to offer help with design ideas.

The Patents Office

State House
66–71 High Holborn
London WC1R 4TP
Tel.: (01) 831 2525

Distance Learning

Council for the Accreditation of Correspondence Colleges

27 Marylebone Road
London NW1 5JS
Tel.: (01) 935 5391

NALGO Correspondence Institute

Nalgo House
1 Mabledon Place
London WC1H 9AJ
Tel.: (01) 388 2366

Runs courses in book-keeping and accounts, also GCSE subjects.

National Extension College

18 Brooklands Avenue
Cambridge CB1 2HN
Tel.: (0223) 316644

Offers a range of business-related courses including communication in business, practical business law, management accounting and, perhaps most relevant of all, a small business course.

Pitmans Correspondence College

Worcester Road
Wimbledon
London SW19 4DS
Tel.: (01) 947 6993

Provides professional and commercial courses, secretarial and general education.

Rapid Results College

Tuition House
St Georges Road
London SW19
Tel.: (01) 946 5138

School of Accountancy and Business Studies

Intertext House
8 Elliot Place
Glasgow G8 8ES
Tel.: (041) 221 2926

Runs professional courses, business and commercial courses.

Health and Safety

The Health and Safety Executive

The Health and Safety Executive has three addresses you can write to for advice and for any queries:

St Hugh's House
Trinity Road
Bootle
Merseyside L20 3QY
Tel.: (051) 951 4000

Baynards House
Westbourne Grove
London W2 4TF
Tel.: (01) 229 3456

Broad Lane
Sheffield
S3 7HQ
Tel.: (0742) 752539

Three important consultants on health and safety are:

British Safety Council

62–64 Chancellors Road
London W6 9RS

Institute of Occupational Safety and Health

222 Uppingham Road
Leicester LE5 0QG
Tel.: (0533) 768424

Royal Society for the Prevention of Accidents

Cannon House
Priory Queensway
Birmingham B4 6BS
Tel.: (021) 200 2461

Market Research

HMSO

49 High Holborn
London WC1V 6HB
Tel.: (01) 211 5656

The Market Research Society

175 Oxford Street
London W1R 1TA
Tel.: (01) 439 2585

The British Market Research Bureau Ltd

Saunders House
53 The Mall
London W5
Tel.: (01) 567 3060

Advertising

The Institute of Practitioners in Advertising

44 Belgrave Square
London SW1X 8QS
Tel.: (01) 235 7020

The Advertising Standards Authority

Brook House
2–16 Torrington Place
London WC1E 7HN
Tel.: (01) 580 5555